Influence: Mastering Life's Most Powerful Skill

Kenneth G. Brown, Ph.D., SPHR®

THE
GREAT
COURSES·

PUBLISHED BY:

THE GREAT COURSES
Corporate Headquarters
4840 Westfields Boulevard, Suite 500
Chantilly, Virginia 20151-2299
Phone: 1-800-832-2412
Fax: 703-378-3819
www.thegreatcourses.com

Kenneth G. Brown, Ph.D., SPHR®
Professor of Management and Organizations
The University of Iowa

P rofessor Kenneth G. Brown is Professor of Management and Organizations and Research Fellow in the Henry B. Tippie College of Business at The University of Iowa. He also serves as Professor of Educational Policy and Leadership Studies in the College of Education. After graduating with university and departmental honors in Psychology from the University of Maryland, College Park, Professor Brown attended Michigan State University, where he earned his M.A. and Ph.D. in Industrial and Organizational Psychology. In 2012, he worked as a visiting scholar at both Monash University and Deakin University in Melbourne, Victoria, Australia.

Professor Brown conducts research on learning and motivation. He also studies the science-practice gap as it relates to everyday management practices. He is coauthor of a textbook entitled *Human Resource Management: Linking Strategy to Practice* and is certified as a Senior Professional in Human Resources (SPHR®). His research appears in many journals and edited books and has been discussed in *The Wall Street Journal*, among other media outlets. For his scholarly work, Professor Brown has received annual research awards from both the American Society for Training and Development and the Society for Human Resource Management. He also has received awards for best paper published in *Human Resource Management* and *Academy of Management Learning and Education*.

Professor Brown is actively involved in service to his profession. He has served on numerous national committees, including an elected term on the Executive Committee of the Human Resources Division of the Academy of Management. He currently serves as editor in chief of the premier educational journal in the business disciplines, *Academy of Management Learning and Education*. He also has served or is currently serving on the editorial boards of *Academy of Management Review, Cornell Hospitality*

Quarterly, Human Resource Development Quarterly, Human Resource Management, Journal of Management, Journal of Management Education, Organization Management Journal, and *Personnel Psychology.*

Professor Brown taught his first university course as an undergraduate student; since that time, he has been recognized for his teaching efforts with a variety of awards. He was twice voted as the Students' Choice for Faculty Excellence in the Tippie College and was selected to give the university's Last Lecture in 2011. He also has won the highest teaching honor bestowed at The University of Iowa, the President and Provost Award for Teaching Excellence. Professor Brown uses a wide variety of teaching methods in his courses, including participation in real-world service-learning projects. His students have worked on projects with many local organizations, including the Iowa Valley Habitat for Humanity ReStore, the Iowa City Animal Care and Adoption Center, the Council for International Visitors to Iowa Cities, and The Crisis Center of Johnson County. ∎

Table of Contents

Table of Contents

LECTURE 11
Developing Negotiation Skills...186

LECTURE 12
Becoming a Transformational Leader..205

SUPPLEMENTAL MATERIAL

Influence: Mastering Life's Most Powerful Skill

Scope:

Influence and persuasion are fundamental to everyday life. From the alarm clock that startles us awake in the morning to the commercial interruptions of our favorite evening television shows, we are bombarded with efforts to get us to do, say, or believe particular things. This series of lectures will help you to better understand influence across the spectrum, from the mundane alarm clock to the symbol-driven political strategy that averted civil war in post-apartheid South Africa.

This course explores the factors that contribute to success stories, such as Nelson Mandela's in South Africa. It illustrates how some people harness the power of influence to achieve worthwhile goals at home, at work, and in their social lives. In addition to positive examples, the course also offers cautionary tales, such as the Ponzi scheme run by Bernie Madoff, because it's crucial to understand the influence tactics used by people who intend to take advantage of us.

The course introduces a model to depict the components of an influence attempt that contribute to its success or failure. The ATTiC model is an acronym representing four fundamental elements: agent, target, tactic, and context. As the course explains, ATTiC is more than an acronym; it is also a useful metaphor. Many factors that determine the success or failure of influence operate outside of conscious awareness. In this way, the four factors are much like the attic of a house—always present, even when the residents aren't thinking about it. In the same way, factors that make us susceptible to influence are built into our basic psychology. By bringing these factors to light, this course not only helps you develop the skills that will make you a more influential person, but it also provides practical guidelines for resisting influence attempts when doing so is in your best interests.

The first seven lectures review research and examples of each component of the ATTiC model. The remaining lectures cover more specific applications of influence, including impression management, sales, public speaking, negotiation, and leadership. In these lectures, we will see how the four elements of influence play out in everyday situations. These lectures also offer suggestions for using your new understanding of influence to achieve better results in these situations. ∎

A Model for Successful Influence
Lecture 1

Everywhere we turn, we find influence—both positive and negative—in action. In this course, we'll explore how some people harness the power of influence to achieve worthwhile goals at home, at work, and in their social lives. But we should never forget that influence can be used against us—that we can be swayed to buy things we don't need and pressured to perform actions we shouldn't. For this reason, we will also analyze cautionary tales related to influence. Our goals in the course will be to develop skills in using influence and to learn to resist outside influence when it's sensible to do so.

Pervasive Influence

- Research psychologist Kevin Dutton claims that we are subjected to influence attempts around 400 times a day! And business author Daniel Pink suggests in his latest book that we're always selling something—even if it's just an idea.

- At first, these claims might seem overstated, but think back over the conversations you had just yesterday. How many times did someone suggest a course of action to you? "Let's remodel the master bath," or "Why don't we eat out tonight?" And don't forget the steady bombardment of advertising. If you count all those pop-up ads that assail you on the Internet, then 400 influence attempts might actually seem low.

- Of course, not every attempt at influence succeeds. Some political campaigns, for instance, excite people and win votes, but others fall flat. In this course, we will examine the mechanisms that contribute to the success or failure of persuasion.

Outcomes of Persuasion
- What are the possible outcomes of an effort at persuasion? A management scholar might identify three: conflict, compliance, and commitment.

- Conflict occurs when the target of your influence resists your ideas or even fights against you. Conflict is, in effect, a failure of influence. Successful influence, on the other hand, results in one of the other two outcomes: compliance or commitment.

- In our day-to-day interactions, we often strive for commitment but will settle for compliance. Commitment means that people buy in completely and internalize what they are being convinced to believe. Often, managers work toward the goal of commitment from their employees—in such areas as customer service or job safety—but will settle for compliance.

Components of an Influence Attempt
- In most influence attempts, we can identify four components that play a critical role in determining success or failure: (1) the agent, that is, the person who is trying to exert influence; (2) the target, the person or group whom the agent is trying to influence; (3) tactics, what an agent says or does to accomplish his or her aims; and (4) the context, the circumstances that shape the interaction of the agent and target. We can remember these components with the acronym ATTiC.

- ATTiC is more than an acronym; it is also a useful metaphor. Many factors that determine the success or failure of influence operate outside of our conscious awareness.
  - Consider the agent, for example—the person who is trying to exert an influence. Some people you meet seem immediately trustworthy or likeable, and you might find their claims and arguments compelling.

In a political speech, ATTiC breaks down as follows: the politician (agent), the crowd of listeners (target), the content and delivery of the speech (tactics), and the setting (context).

o   Bob Cialdini, author of the bestseller *Influence: Science and Practice*, argues that influence often happens in a "click-whirr" fashion. It's as if a switch was clicked, and an automatic routine whirrs into action. Something about the agent or, perhaps, the tactic quickly starts a process that ends with compliance or commitment, without any intervening conscious thought.

o   In this way, the four factors are much like the attic of your house. Your attic is always present even when you aren't thinking about it. In the same way, factors that make us susceptible to influence are built into our basic psychology and often operate outside of our conscious awareness.

o   The better you understand the natural mechanisms that result in influence, the more you can use them to your advantage and correct for them when someone is using them against you.

The Successful Agent

- According to Cialdini, "liking" is a major principle of successful influence. In other words, an agent's success is often based on how well he or she is liked by other people. When people like you, they are more likely to listen to your arguments and be convinced by them. They are also more likely to want to please you and go along with your wants and desires.

- One important pathway to liking is perceived similarity. When people see you as similar to them in some fashion, they immediately—and almost automatically—like you more.
  - In one study published by Professor Jerry Burger and his colleagues from Santa Clara University, 62 percent of female undergraduate participants agreed to help a fellow student with whom they thought they shared a birthday, compared to 34 percent who agreed to help when they believed they and the other student had different birthdays.

  - In a similar study, Professor Burger found that students contributed more than twice as much to a cause ($2.07 versus $1.00) when they thought they shared the same name as the requestor.

  - In these studies, participants were not aware that they had been influenced by the incidental similarity between themselves and the person making a request. The increase in liking and helping happened outside of their awareness, hidden away in the ATTiC of their minds, so to speak.

- These studies suggest that agents can be more effective influencers when they tap into the power of incidental similarity and liking. If you want to be more influential, you might think about highlighting similarities between you and the people with whom you're talking.

The Receptive Target

- Throughout this course, we'll look at many characteristics that might make a target more receptive to influence. One that might be surprising is the target's home country.

- Rod Bond and Peter Smith, both from the University of Sussex in England, examined 133 compliance studies drawn from 17 different countries. Their analysis revealed that studies conducted in collectivist countries found higher rates of conformity to group opinion than studies conducted in individualist countries. In other words, people from collectivist societies seem to be more susceptible to group influence than people from individualist societies.

- University of Illinois scholar Harry Triandis describes individualist and collectivist societies as follows: In an individualist culture, it is acceptable for a person to place more importance on personal goals than collective goals. In collectivist cultures, it is expected that a person will place more importance on collective goals than personal ones. Collectivist countries include China, Korea, Japan, Brazil, Argentina, and Egypt. Individualist countries include Germany, Canada, the United States, Australia, Holland, and England.

Tactics That Work

- As we all know, some influence tactics work better than others. Imagine, for example, that you want to influence your boss to promote you. What tactics work best—focusing on the job or focusing on your supervisor?

- Business professors Tim Judge and Bob Bretz found that supervisor-focused influence had a much more positive effect; those who focused their influence on the job had lower salaries and fewer promotions than those who focused on their supervisors.

- In other words, tactics that make your boss like you may be more important than tactics that demonstrate your competence.

Taking Advantage of Context

- Context may include what has happened recently or what is happening right now around you. Most compelling is what other people are doing. We all have a natural tendency to make sense of the world based on how others react to it. If you hear a strange sound while walking through a store, you look around. If no one else seems concerned, you will conclude that all is well and continue on your way.

- One of the most classic psychology experiments of the 20th century related to context was conducted by Solomon Asch at Swarthmore College.
  - In Asch's study, a participant was brought into a room with a number of research confederates. The participant was told that he was participating in a study of visual acuity. Two large cards were shown to the group. On one card was a single line—the target line. On the other card was a set of three lines of varying length.

  - Each person in the room was asked, "Which of the three lines matches the target the line?" When the majority of the confederates selected the wrong line, one-third of participants also gave the incorrect answer. They reported something they knew to be false, just to agree with others in the room.

  - In another set of studies, Asch varied the number of confederates who identified the wrong line. When only one confederate gave an incorrect answer, the number of errors made by subjects was quite low. But the subjects' error rate increased when two or three confederates identified the wrong line. Further increases in the number of mistaken confederates added a little to the error rate but not much. Thus, three seems to be a magic number for bring about conformity.

Application: The ATTiC Concept

- In this lecture, we've begun to explore the components of the ATTiC acronym—agent, target, tactics, and context—and we've begun to see how these components help determine whether a particular influence attempt results in conflict, compliance, or commitment.

- To help you consolidate this information, try this suggestion the next time you find yourself being convinced by someone else: Stop and think about what's going on in the ATTiC. Are there factors outside your awareness that are having an effect on you? For example, is someone arguing that you should believe a certain argument because other people do? If so, imagine an equal number of people advancing the opposite argument. This approach may help you to think more critically about the issue yourself.

- Another activity to try is this: The next time you're out to dinner, try to leverage similarity to get better service. Ask your server a few questions to find some similarity and point it out. If Professor Burger's results hold up, you might get a little extra attention during your meal.

Suggested Reading

Cialdini, *Influence: Science and Practice.*

Dutton, *Split-Second Persuasion.*

Activities to Try

1. The next time you find yourself being convinced of something, stop and ask yourself: What's going on in the ATTiC? Is there something going on outside of your awareness that is having an effect on you? Becoming aware may help you to think more critically about the issue.

2. The next time you're out to dinner, try to leverage similarity to get better service. Ask your server a few questions to find some similarity and point it out. If research results hold up, you might just get a little extra attention during your meal.

Real-World Influence Scenario

Imagine that you and three business associates are on a trip in a large city. Your work is done for the day, and you're enjoying a meal at a restaurant together. You've agreed to use the remainder of your free night to spend some time together, but you haven't decided what to do next. Your preference is to see a musical that's been on your wish list for more than a year. Another member of the group proposes a walking tour. How can you apply ATTiC to influence your colleagues to see the show you would like to see?

- **Agent**: If you're well-liked, you may have already convinced your colleagues to see the show. If you have to work a little harder than that, highlight similarities, such as shared interests, among you.

- **Target**: Find out whether your colleagues are from collectivist or individualist cultures. If they are more collectivist in orientation, they may be more likely to go along to preserve harmony in the group. If they are more individualistic, you may have to work a bit harder to convince them.

- **Tactics**: Remember, tactics that make your targets like you may be more important than other considerations. Compliment your colleagues on their good taste, and explain why that good taste would result in their enjoyment of the show!

- **Context**: Having most of the group on your side will dramatically increase your chance of winning over the colleague who is proposing an alternative plan. If possible, you can even try to win over the other members of the group in advance.

A Model for Successful Influence
Lecture 1—Transcript

Anywhere you turn you'll find influence in action, a fast-talking stock broker persuades a couple, near retirement, to sink their entire life savings into a Ponzi scheme; a CEO pressures an accounting officer to falsify financial statements; a terrorist cell recruits a frustrated youth and convinces him to strap explosives to his chest. But for all the horrible things we can be talked into, people can also use influence to achieve fantastic results. Think of the firefighter who talks the depressed man out of jumping or the dynamic teacher who inspires her struggling student to stay in school. And then, there are the truly great triumphs of influence. Consider the remarkable story of Nelson Mandela, chronicled in numerous books and movies. How can one person use his powers of persuasion to prevent an all-out civil war? Nelson Mandela showed us how.

In this course we're going to look at the factors that contribute to success stories like Mandela's. We're going to explore how some people harness the power of influence to achieve worthwhile goals at home, at work, and in their social lives. But, we're also going to analyze the cautionary tales; we should never forget that influence can be used against us, that we can be swayed to buy things we don't need and pressured to perform actions we really shouldn't. So in addition to developing your influence skills, one important goal of this course is to give you information that will help you resist outside influence when it's in your best interest to do so, because, let's face it, influence is pervasive in our daily lives. In fact, research psychologist Kevin Dutton makes the claim that we are subjected to influence attempts somewhere near 400 times a day—400. And business author Dan Pink suggests in his latest book that we are always selling something, even if it's just an idea. That might seem overstated, but think back over yesterday; how many conversations did you have where someone suggested a course of action to you? Why don't we eat there tonight? Or, hey, let's remodel the master bath. Or, I'd like to get a second dog. I had that last conversation a while back, was convinced, and spent weeks wiping messes off my floor.

Then there's the steady bombardment of advertising. If you count all those pop-up ads that assail you whenever you browse the web these days, then

400 influence attempts might actually seem too low. And what about politics? I live in the state of Iowa, and we have candidates trying to convince us that they're qualified to be president of the United States for what seems like two full years leading up to the primaries. Like it or not, it seems that someone is always trying to persuade us to do something. Of course, not every attempt at influence succeeds. Some of those Iowa campaigns, for example, the speeches, advertisements, endorsements, and rallies, some of them really excite people and win votes, but others fall completely flat. Why is that? Well, we are going to spend a lot of time in this course examining the mechanisms that contribute to the success or failure of persuasion.

But first, let's take a moment to pin down what we mean by success and failure in the first place. If I'm trying to convince you to do something, what are the possible outcomes of my effort? Ask any management scholar that question, and she'll probably identify three possible outcomes: conflict, compliance, and commitment—the three Cs. If you've raised a child through adolescence and been told, "you are not the boss of me," then you have encountered conflict. Conflict is when the target of your influence resists your ideas and even fights against you. It is, in effect, a failure of influence. Successful influence, on the other hand, results in one of the other two outcomes: compliance or commitment. In our day-to-day interactions, we often strive for commitment but will settle for compliance. Commitment means that people buy in completely and internalize what they're being convinced to believe. With my own children, I want them to clean their rooms and help with the dishes and would prefer that they commit to it, that they do so cheerfully, and of their own free will. But, as we work towards that goal, I will settle for compliance. When I ask, they do it. Many managers I work with feel the same way about their employees. When it comes to customer service, job safety, and other desired work behaviors, commitment is the ultimate goal, but compliance at least means the employees are doing what they're asked when they are asked.

So now that we have a more precise way of talking about success and failure, let's look at the factors that determine whether a particular influence attempt yields conflict, compliance, or commitment. If you step back to think about an influence situation, a political speech in small-town Iowa, for example, you'll quickly realize that there are quite a few moving pieces that could have an impact on the outcome. To organize these pieces into a useful scheme, we can identify four basic components that play a critical role. First, there's the politician; then there's the content and delivery of the speech itself; next is the crowd; and finally, there is the setting. And really the four components that contribute to the success or failure of this political speech can be detected in almost every influence attempt.

So let's give each of these four components a more general name that we can apply to any situation where someone tries to persuade or influence others. First, let's call the politician the agent; in any situation, the agent is the person who is trying to influence someone else. Second, let's call the crowd the target; in any situation, the target is the person or group whom the agent is trying to influence. Third, we can generalize the content and delivery of the speech itself by referring to tactics. Every influence attempt involves a set of tactics; in other words, what an agent says or does to accomplish her aims. Fourth, and finally, the setting of that Iowa speech is nothing other than the context. Agents and targets don't operate in a vacuum; they're surrounded by circumstances that shape their interactions, that's context.

So we have agent, target, tactics, and context. You'll want to remember those four key components of influence because we'll be returning to them time and time again throughout the course. To make them easier to remember, I've created an acronym from the first letter of each component: A, T, T and C. Just like the Apple corporation, let's make liberal use of the letter i to put a vowel. Adding the i we get ATTiC. If you want to know why a particular influence attempt results in conflict, commitment, or compliance, look in the ATTiC. ATTiC is more than an acronym, though. It's a useful metaphor. Many factors that determine the success or failure of influence operate outside of our conscious awareness. Take the agent, for example, the person who's trying to influence us. Sometimes we meet someone and find her immediately trustworthy or likeable and then find her claims and arguments so compelling.

Bob Cialdini, author of the worldwide bestseller, *Influence: Science and Practice*, talks about influence often happening in a "click-whirr" fashion. It's as if a switch were clicked, and then an automatic routine whirrs into action. Something about the agent, or maybe it's the tactic, quickly kicks in, a psychological process that ends up with compliance or commitment without any intervening conscious thought. In this way, the four factors are very much like the attic of your house. Your attic is always there, and it's always doing what it does, even when you aren't thinking about it. In the same way, factors that make us susceptible to influence are built into our basic psychology and often operate outside of our conscious awareness. That's why it's important for you to learn as much as possible about agent, target, tactics, and context. The better you understand the natural mechanisms that result in influence, the more you can use them to your advantage and correct for them when someone is using them against you.

To familiarize you with the ATTiC concept, I'm going to make use of a real-world scenario that we can revisit throughout the rest of this lecture. Here's the situation. Imagine you and three business associates are on a trip into the city. Your work is done for the day and you're enjoying a meal at a restaurant together. You've agreed to use the remainder of your free night to spend more time together, but you haven't decided what to do next. Your preference is to see a musical that's been on your wish list for over a year. Another member of the group proposes a walking tour. What are the factors that determine whether you are able to successfully influence your colleagues and see the show you really want to see? We're going to answer that question in terms of the four corners of the ATTiC—agent, target, tactics, and context. First, though, let me say a brief word about ethics. For some of you, "influence" may sound like a bad word, and as we'll see in future lectures, it does, indeed, have a dark side. There are people who use tricks and lies to get what they want. It's important to state up front that there are also ethical and honest ways to persuade others, and through this course, I will encourage you to stick to these ways.

With that in mind, let's get back to our question. What factors come into play when I'm trying to influence my colleagues to see that musical downtown? Let's begin by finding out what research has to say about the A in our acronym, the agent. A few moments ago I mentioned Bob Cialdini, who is an emeritus professor from Arizona State University; according to Cialdini, liking is a major principle of successful influence. In other words, an agent's success often comes down to how well he or she is liked by other people, the target, in particular. When people like you, they are more likely to listen to your arguments and be convinced by them. They're also more likely to want to please you and go along with what it is you want or desire, but, what makes people like an agent in the first place? Obviously, there are many pathways to liking, but one very important one is perceived similarity. When people see you as similar to them in some fashion, they automatically, and I might add, almost immediately, like you more. To illustrate, let me explain the results of two studies published by Professor Jerry Burger and his colleagues from Santa Clara University.

In study one, female undergraduates were brought into a room one at a time and told to fill out a survey while sitting next to another student. This second student was actually working with the experimenter. She is what social psychologists call a research confederate. As part of the experiment, the confederate surreptitiously glances at the participant's survey to learn her birthday. After the survey was completed, the experimenter asked a series of questions to both women at once, eventually coming around to asking their birthdays. The research confederate would always speak up first. Half of the time the confederate would give a birthday that differed from the participant; we'll call that the control condition. The other half of the time, the confederate would claim to have the exact same birthday. After questioning the students, the experimenter would leave the room, and at this point, the confederate would ask the participant for a favor. She explained that an English class assignment required her to find someone she did not know to critique an essay she'd written. She said, I wonder if you could read this eight-page essay for me and give me one-page of written feedback on whether my arguments are persuasive and why? In the control condition, just over one-third agreed to help, 34 percent. In the same-birthday condition, nearly two thirds agreed to help, 62 percent. In other words, nearly twice as many subjects agreed to provide feedback on that essay when they thought the requester was similar to them in some fashion, in this case, because they happened to share the same birthday.

In Professor Burger's second study, the researchers wanted to be sure there wasn't something unique about discovering that someone shares the same birthday. So this time, participants were introduced to another student, again, a confederate, wearing a nametag and holding a poster. On the poster was a picture of a young lady with a caption including her name and a quote.

In one condition the confederate's nametag showed a name identical to the participant's. This is equivalent to a shared birthday; this time it's a shared name. But there were also two other conditions. In one, the person in the poster had a name identical to the participant's name. This allowed the researchers to see if the basic experience of encountering similarity makes people more helpful or likely to comply. In the final condition there was no name similarity on either the poster or the confederate's nametag. So, research participants experienced one of three conditions: having the same name with the person holding the sign, having the same name with the person pictured on the sign, or not having any name similarity.

In all conditions, the confederate holding the sign asked the participant for a favor, in this case, a donation to the cause described on the poster. Would the student donate? The study sought to see how much people gave in each condition. Average giving in dollars was as follows. With no name similarity, $1.00; the same name with the person on the poster, a little less, $0.81; the same name with the person requesting the donation, $2.07; again, the perceived similarity between agent and target makes a huge difference. Comparing no name similarity to the condition where the requester has the same name as the participant, we see a doubling of giving. Study one showed a doubling of compliance, helping with that essay based on shared birthday, and study two showed a doubling of giving based on a shared name.

In these studies, participants were not at all aware that they'd been influenced by the incidental similarity between them and the person making the request. If you had asked the participants, were you influenced by the person's birthday or by their name, they would respond blankly, "Why would I be?" The increase in liking and helping happens outside of awareness, hidden away in the attic of their minds, so to speak. These studies suggest that agents could be more effective influencers when they tap into the power of incidental similarity and liking. So, if you want to be more influential, you might think about highlighting similarities between you and the people you're talking to. Take the scenario where you're trying to influence your colleague to see a show. If you're well liked, then perhaps you've already convinced her. Even so, you might try to find and highlight some similarity that you share. Maybe you both like gardening, call attention to that and enjoy the conversation that the similarity produces.

Now that we've discussed the agent, let's move to target, which in our scenario is the business colleague you're trying to influence to see the musical. What is a characteristic of your colleague that might make her more receptive to your influence? Well, there are many target characteristics that we'll address in this course, but here's one that might surprise you. Where is your colleague from? Rod Bond and Peter Smith, both from the University of Sussex, in England, examined 133 compliance studies drawn from 17 different countries. What they found is fascinating. Their analysis revealed that studies conducted in collectivist countries found higher rates of conformity to group opinion than studies conducted in individualist countries. In other words, people from collectivist societies seem to be more susceptible to group influence than people from individualist societies.

But what do we mean by collectivist and individualist societies? University of Illinois scholar, Harry Triandis describes it this way; in an individualist culture, it is acceptable for a person to place more importance of personal goals than collective goals. In collectivist cultures, the opposite is true. It is expected that a person will place more importance on the collective goals rather than the personal ones. Countries with collectivist cultures include China, Korea, Japan, Brazil, Argentina, and Egypt. Countries with individualist cultures include Germany, Canada, the United States, Australia, Holland, and England. So, returning to our scenario at the restaurant table, we should ask, where is your colleague from. If she is from a collectivist culture, then she may be more likely to go along just to preserve harmony in the group, but if she is more individualistic in orientation, you may have to work a bit harder to convince her.

Remember our acronym, ATTiC? So far we've discussed the A, agent, and the first T, target. Now it's time to discuss our second T, tactics. Some influence tactics work better than others, as you've probably witnessed watching some people get their way with ease, while others really struggle. Let's say, for example, that you want to influence your boss to promote you. What tactics work best? Business professors Tim Judge and Bob Bretz wondered whether focusing on the job, doing a good job at work and letting others know about it, was more important than focusing on your supervisor, agreeing with and praising your supervisor. Judge and Bretz asked graduates from two large universities to complete a survey. The survey assessed two things. First, how the participants genuinely influenced others at work, and second, what career outcomes they'd experienced, including current salary and number of promotions. One might imagine that job-focused influence would lead a person to be perceived as competent and supervisor-focused influence would lead a person to be well liked. So which is more important? Controlling for other potential causes of career success, the researchers found that focusing on your supervisor had a much more positive effect than anything else. So, those who focused their influence on the job actually had lower salaries and fewer promotions than those who focused on their supervisor. These results suggest that tactics that make your boss like you may be more important than tactics that demonstrate your competence on the job. Returning to our situation, colleagues in the city deciding what to do, what tactic might you use? You might compliment your colleague on her good taste and explain why that good taste would result in her enjoyment of the show you want to see.

Finally, in our tour of the ATTiC, we come to context. Context may include what has happened recently or what is happening right now around you. Most compelling is what other people are doing. We all have a natural tendency to make sense of the world based on how others react to it. If, for example, you hear an uncertain sound while you're walking through a store, you'll look around. If no one else seems concerned, you'll conclude that all is well and continue on your way. One of the most classic psychology experiments of the 20th century was conducted by Solomon Asch at Swarthmore College. The paradigm for Asch's study was simple. A participant was brought into a room with a number of research confederates. He was told that he was participating in a study of visual acuity. Two large cards were shown to the group. On one card was a single line, the target line. The other card was a set of three lines of varying length. Each person in the room was then asked, which of the three lines on this card matches the target line on that card? The experimenter always began with the research confederates, asking each to report which line matched. This is where things got interesting.

In some cases, all the confederates reported the correct answer, but in other cases, they deliberately gave the wrong answer. So what did participants do when everyone stated out loud an opinion that disagreed with what their own eyes were telling them? When the majority in the room claimed the wrong line matched, one-third of the participants would go along and also state out loud the incorrect answer. That means that one-third looked carefully and reported something they knew to be false just to agree with others in the room. That's the power of context. In another set of studies conducted by Asch, he varied the number of experimental confederates who identified the wrong line. When only one confederate stated an incorrect line, the number of errors made by subjects was quite low. The subject's error rate increased when two confederates identified the wrong line and then got even higher when three gave an incorrect answer. Further increases—four, five and six—added a little to error rate, but not much. So it seems that three is a magic number.

There is a Chinese phrase, three people produce a tiger. This is ancient wisdom that captures what Asch discovered in his studies. The parable behind the saying goes a bit like this. The state official, Pang Cong, worried that people would slander him and ruin his favor with the king. To prevent this, he asked the king to imagine a scenario. Suppose, king, that a peasant came to you and reported that a tiger was roaming the busy streets of the market. Would you believe him? The king, of course, said there was no way he would believe. A tiger would never wander out of the forest into a crowded market. Pang Cong continued. What if two peasants reported seeing the tiger? The king said he would begin to wonder but would not believe. Pang Cong then asked, what if three people say they saw the tiger? The king replied that in this case he would believe.

Pang Cong gently reminded the king that the notion of a live tiger in a crowded market was absurd, yet when repeated by numerous people it began to seem real. It is clear there is no tiger in the market, Pang Cong would say, yet three people saying so produces a tiger. Why should the king believe something so unlikely? Of course, what happened in this story was that Pang Cong was talked about badly after he left, and the king refused to ever see him again. Was the king correct to listen to the slanderous talk, or was the official wise in warning against it? It's hard to know, but the saying, three people produce a tiger, makes clear the natural process that occurs when we are influenced to conform to a crowd opinion.

Let's circle back to the example we've been using throughout the lecture. How might context work in your favor as your business group tries to finalize its plans for the evening? It should be clear from Asch's studies that having most of the group on your side will dramatically increase your chance of winning over your colleague who's proposing an alternative idea. You might even consider winning over other members of the group in advance so that when the time for the big decision comes, you have the crowd on your side all claiming, hey, we will have a great time if we go see that show.

The people around you are a big part of the C, or context, of influence. In this lecture we've also begun to explore the other three components of our ATTiC acronym—agent, target, and tactics. And we've begun to see how all of these components help determine whether a particular influence attempt results in conflict, compliance, or commitment. To help you consolidate this information and to put it to good use, I'd like to offer two suggestions for things you can try on your own. Influence is a really practical topic, and I think you will find many opportunities to apply what I present to your everyday routines and interactions.

First, next time you find yourself being convinced by someone, stop and think. What's going on in the ATTiC? Is there something going on outside of my awareness that's having an effect on me? For example, is someone arguing that you should believe something because other people do? Do you find yourself being persuaded? If so, make a mental note, and you can correct for that by imagining an equal number of people advancing the opposite argument. This may help you to think more critically about the issue for yourself.

The second activity I suggest is this. Next time you're out for dinner try to leverage similarity to get better service. If incidental similarity results in more helping and giving as the studies we've talked about suggest, then finding similarity with someone waiting on your table might just get you a bit more help than usual. So, ask your server a few questions and look for some similarity, and then, point it out. Hey, I'm from Columbia, Maryland too, or, that's so funny, I love tomatoes too. If professor Burger's results hold up, then you might just get a little extra help the rest of the dinner.

In our next lecture we'll take a closer look at agents, the A in our ATTiC. If you've ever met someone who seemed to possess some kind of magic that helps them win people over, then join me next time to find out just what that magic is and even to learn how to get some of it for yourself.

Characteristics of Influential Agents
Lecture 2

In the last lecture, we introduced the ATTiC concept, our acronym and metaphor for the four key factors that contribute to the success or failure of any influence attempt. In this lecture, we'll take a closer look at the A in ATTiC—the agent, or the person who is trying to influence someone else. We'll identify some of the most important characteristics of the influential agent, and we'll explore how those characteristics play out in real-world situations.

Physical Attractiveness
- In the last lecture, we saw that similarity led to liking, which allowed agents to be more persuasive. Another characteristic that leads lead to liking and more effective influence is physical attractiveness.

- University of Texas Professor Judy Langlois and her colleagues examined research results across hundreds of studies testing to see whether perceptions of physical attractiveness varied across people and cultures and whether judgments of attractiveness correlate with other judgments about people. For example, when someone is more attractive, is that person also judged to be more intelligent?
  - Across 67 studies, the researchers found fairly high agreement about what constituted more and less physically attractive individuals. Agreement was even high across ethnicities and cultures and for judgments of children and adults.

  - Factors associated with physical attractiveness, regardless of culture, include symmetrical and proportionately balanced features, large eyes, a small nose, and prominent cheekbones.

- Langlois and her colleagues also looked across many studies to see whether children and adults judged as attractive would also be seen as having other positive characteristics.

o They examined judgments of academic competence, adjustment, interpersonal competence, and social appeal for children and adults.

o Across every one of these dimensions, 75 percent of attractive children were judged to be above the mean, while only 25 percent of unattractive children were judged to be above the mean. In adults, these figures were 63 percent above the mean for attractive faces, and 37 percent above the mean for unattractive faces.

- Further, Langlois and colleagues examined studies measuring how people treat more and less attractive people. They found that attractive children and adults receive more attention, cooperation, and care from other people than those judged unattractive.

- These results have important ramifications for influence. Attractive agents have an advantage over everyone else because the targets of their influence will, without consciously deciding to do so, think positively of them and be more likely to cooperate. All other factors being equal, an attractive agent is more likely to be persuasive.

- In addition to the effects of general attractiveness, other research suggests that specific facial features contribute to judgments of an agent's trustworthiness.
  o Professor Constantin Rezlescu of University College London and colleagues across the United Kingdom and the United States used a virtual money-lending game to show how much we trust people with different facial features.

  o The average amount lent to people with "trustworthy" faces was almost 50 percent more than that lent to people with "untrustworthy" faces. Even when given negative credit information about the people to whom they were lending, subjects lent slightly more to those with trustworthy faces.

- The faces used in the study were created through detailed simulation work by Alexander Todorov at Princeton. Todorov's mathematical models created a somewhat feminine-looking trustworthy face—narrower, with wider eyes, arching eyebrows, and a mouth that curves up at the sides—along with a more masculine-looking untrustworthy face—wider, with a larger nose and eyebrows, and a mouth that curves down at the sides.

- One explanation for our tendency to make snap judgments of people's trustworthiness based on facial features comes from evolutionary theory. As social animals, humans need to make quick judgments about potential threats among the people with whom we interact. Thus, fast processing of heavily masculine features that are commonly associated with aggression leads to a judgment that someone is a risk and should not be trusted.

The Three Cs

- Of course, how you look isn't all that matters in your ability to influence others. We can all think of examples of average-looking or even below-average-looking leaders who have won over a company or even a country. What have these agents done over time to build credibility and trust with their targets of influence?
  - First, such leaders have ability—skills and competencies that allow them to do things effectively. In other words, trustworthy people are competent.

  - Second, trustworthy people are benevolent or caring.

  - Third, they have integrity—they abide by a set of clear and sensible principles. In other words, trustworthy people are consistent.

- To lay the groundwork for future success as an agent of influence, practice these three Cs: competence, caring, and consistency.

- This model allows us to move beyond initial impressions and offers specific suggestions for you to develop a reputation for trustworthiness. Any agent who wishes to influence other people can work to correct any misperceptions that occur as a result of facial features or other factors outside of the agent's control.

Group Identification

- The assumption that an agent and a target are "on the same team" can also influence judgments. In fact, there's a long history of research in social psychology about the powerful effects of being placed on the same team.

- One of the most famous of these experiments was conducted by Muzafer Sherif in 1954. Sherif took 22 boys, ages 11 and 12, to a summer camp at Robbers Cave State Park in Oklahoma. The boys were split into two camps—the Rattlers and the Eagles—and, over the course of two weeks, went through three phases of an experiment.
  - o In the first phase, the teams worked independently, and the relationships among the boys were studied. In the second phase, the groups were introduced to each other and asked to

© Fuse/Thinkstock.

Social psychology research shows that we are more likely to trust and listen to someone who is perceived to be a teammate, whether in sports or in business.

compete in a series of contests. In the third phase, the groups were brought together and given tasks at which they had to collaborate.

- o During the second phase, a variety of conflicts emerged between the two groups. Each group raided the other's cabins; the boys cursed each other and fought.

- o After the contests were over, the boys were asked to rate the characteristics of each group. Not surprisingly, they rated their own group favorably and the other group unfavorably.

- In everyday work or school situations, we don't typically find overt competition between groups, but does the general process of bias toward the ingroup and against the outgroup occur in these settings also? In terms of influence, is someone on your own team more likely to be trusted?
  - o Social psychologist Henri Tajfel and his colleagues were interested in whether more neutral situations might lead to the same kinds of intergroup conflict. Rather than inducing competition, as Sherif had done, Tajfel simply grouped people together arbitrarily and then observed how subjects treated and rated their ingroups versus an outgroup.

  - o The findings suggest that a mere sense of shared group membership can increase liking and trust. Agents who are most influential are those who have some overlap in group membership with their targets.

Charisma
- Charisma, which involves saying the right things in the right way, is often considered a rare and magical quality of leadership that arouses loyalty and enthusiasm. However, a growing body of evidence suggests that with training, anyone can become more charismatic.

- A study by John Antonakis, Marika Fenley, and Sue Liechti, all from the University of Lausanne, compared managers who received charisma training to those who did not. Although the groups were similar before training, the trained group showed higher levels of charisma after training, according to their colleagues at work.
  - The training included tips on charismatic speaking and specific feedback for the trainees on the ways in which they were and were not charismatic.

  - Thus, charisma isn't some magical inborn ability; it is something that anyone can develop with feedback and practice.

- *The Charisma Myth* by Olivia Fox Cabane offers helpful advice on developing charisma, including the idea that "charisma begins in the mind." She provides a series of exercises to help people become more confident and rid themselves of physical and psychological discomfort.
  - Cabane notes that charismatic people take charge of situations and change them to work in their favor. Reducing your own physical discomfort in a situation prevents you from communicating a series of nonverbal messages that undermine any sense that you're charismatic.

  - For psychological discomfort, Cabane suggests an exercise called responsibility transfer. When you begin to get anxious, follow these steps: (1) sit comfortably and relax, (2) take a few deep breaths, (3) imagine a benevolent, caring presence, and (4) imagine lifting the weight of everything you are anxious about and placing it in the hands of this presence.

Application: Charisma Training
- The next time you meet someone new, make sure you are both comfortable. Get the setting right so that you can focus your attention on getting to know the person, rather than worrying about being too hot or cold or dealing with other physical discomforts.

- Next, try one of Cabane's training tools to improve nonverbal behaviors.
  - Begin by adopting the body language of someone who is depressed, slumping your shoulders and hanging your head. Maintaining that position, try to imagine being excited. You may find that it's difficult to conjure excitement in this posture.

  - Next, do the opposite; smile and raised your arms in the air as if you've just won a jackpot. Maintain that position and try to feel depressed.

  - This exercise may help remind you that the mind reads the body and allows it to guide mood. Smiling and standing up straight may actually help you feel more confident! Do this exercise before you head into a meeting or conversation in which you are trying to influence someone—it may give you the extra boost you need.

Suggested Reading

Cabane, *The Charisma Myth.*

Sherif, Harvey, White, Hood, and Sherif, *Intergroup Conflict and Cooperation.*

Activities to Try

1. The next time you meet someone new, make sure you are both comfortable. Get the setting right so that you can focus your attention on getting to know the person, rather than worrying about physical discomforts.

2. Adopt the body language of someone who is depressed: Slump your shoulders and hang your head. Then, keeping that position, try to imagine being excited. Now, do the opposite: Put a smile on your face and raise your arms in the air as if you've just won the big game or a jackpot. Maintain that position and try to feel depressed. Doing this

exercise a few times may help remind you that the mind allows the body to guide mood.

Real-World Influence Scenario

On the first day of a new job, your boss says to you, "You look a lot like my ex-husband." Then she adds sarcastically, "I guess I'll have to get used to that." For reasons that have nothing to do with you, you are starting off in hole. To use a budgeting analogy, you're starting out with a trust deficit.

Your best bet to develop trust in this situation is to remember the three Cs. Work hard to build knowledge and be **competent** at your job; look after your boss's interests and be **caring**; and demonstrate a concern for fairness and be **consistent** in how you make decisions. If you pursue these qualities vigorously, you can increase your trustworthiness and the chances that your boss will trust you with greater responsibility and a promotion in the future. In other words, by building your trustworthiness, you create greater opportunity to wield your influence in the workplace.

Characteristics of Influential Agents
Lecture 2—Transcript

Imagine you are just sitting down to dinner at home, savoring the smell of one of your favorite meals. You pick up your fork to get that first bite, and the doorbell rings and rings. You put down the fork and reluctantly walk away from the meal and take a look at who's standing at your door. Who is it? you ask. It's someone conducting a door-to-door survey. You think, seriously? Visiting during my dinner hour? But the person begins to talk, and somehow, miraculously, you're taken in and find yourself not only answering the questions, but also happily chatting away with this visitor. Who could cause you to abandon your favorite meal and answer a survey? What is it about some people that makes them capable of captivating, even pulling you away from something you'd rather be doing?

In our last lecture, we introduced the concept of ,ATTiC, my acronym and metaphor for the four key factors that contribute to success or failure of influence. Can you remember what those four factors are? That's right, agent, target, tactics and context. In this lecture we're going to take a closer look at the A in ATTiC, the agent or person who's trying to influence someone else. We'll also identify some of the most important characteristics of the influential agent, and we'll explore how those characteristics play out in real-world situations.

Let's review what we learned in Lecture 1 about agent characteristics. We discussed liking; incidental similarity made a difference. Similarity led to liking, which allowed agents, in effect, to be more persuasive. What other characteristics of people lead to liking and more effective influence? Let's start with an agent characteristic that's literally right in front of your eyes but that you may not associate with influence. I'm talking about beauty, physical attractiveness. We often hear beauty is in the eye of the beholder, and it is true that people have different tastes and preferences for a wide variety of things, which is why people like different foods, and cars, and houses, and cell phones, and clothing. But when it comes to people, what does research say about our perceptions of beauty and how it relates to influence?

University of Texas professor Judy Langlois and her colleagues examined research results across hundreds of studies, testing to see whether perceptions of physical attractiveness varied across people and cultures, and whether judgments of attractiveness correlate with other judgments about people. For example, when someone is more attractive, is that person also judged to be more intelligent? Across 67 studies, they found fairly high agreement about what constituted more and less physically attractive individuals. Agreement was even high across ethnicities, and cultures, and for judgments of children, as well as adults. What are those characteristics? Research suggests that having symmetrical, proportionally balanced features leads to greater attractiveness, regardless of culture. Other features associated with beauty include large eyes, a small nose, and prominent cheekbones.

Langlois and her colleagues also looked across many studies to see whether children and adults judged as attractive would also be seen as having other positive characteristics. They examined judgments of academic competence, adjustment, interpersonal competence, and social appeal for children and for adults. And they found across every single one of these dimensions that 75 percent of attractive children were judged to be above the mean. In comparison, only 25 percent of unattractive children were judged to be above the mean. If attractiveness didn't matter, both of these numbers should be 50 percent. In adults, 63 percent of attractive faces were above the mean, and only 37 percent of the unattractive were judged above the mean. Langlois and her colleagues also examined studies measuring how people treat more or less attractive people. And what they found is that attractive children and adults are treated more favorably than unattractive, basically. They receive more attention, cooperation, and care from other people. These results have important ramifications for influence. Attractive agents have an advantage over other people as the targets of their influence will, without consciously deciding to do so, think positively of them and be more likely to cooperate. An attractive agent is more likely to be persuasive, all else equal.

Because research finds clear differences in how people are perceived and treated based on looks, researchers have continued to examine features of agents' faces. And research now suggests that, in addition to effects of general attractiveness, there are other specific facial features that contribute to judgments of an agent's trustworthiness. Professor Constantin Rezlescu of University College London and colleagues across the U.K. and U.S. designed a clever study to show how much we trust people with different facial features. The researchers used a game where people lend virtual money to a partner they see on a computer screen. Participants were shown a face on the computer screen, asked to read a bit of text, and given a choice of how much money to lend. Each person looked at a few different faces and made a series of lending decisions.

What were the results? Well, the average amount invested in an untrustworthy face was 44 virtual pounds, while trustworthy faces attracted 62 virtual pounds, almost 50 percent more. Participants were not necessarily aware that they were using this facial information to determine how much they lend. But what happens if people know the past history of the people to whom they're lending money? When given written information on the screen about how the person had behaved in the past, had this person given a good or bad rate of return on past lending, people lent more money to those with good history; that's rational, 67 virtual pounds, as compared to 21 virtual pounds for those with a bad history. But if you had a trustworthy face, you received a bump of about 2 pounds. So even knowing a negative past history, a trustworthy face makes a difference. We just can't help but be influenced by an agent's looks.

The faces used in this study were actually created through detailed simulation work by Alexander Todorov at Princeton University. Todorov and his colleagues were able to mathematically model faces that vary along a dimension of trustworthiness. What do these faces look like? A trustworthy face is narrower with wider eyes, arching eyebrows, and a mouth that curves up at the sides. This type of face has what many would consider to be a feminine look. An untrustworthy face is wider, with a larger nose, and eyebrows and mouth that curve down at the sides. This face has more of a masculine, tough-guy look. Why would we make snap judgments of people's trustworthiness based on facial features? One explanation is evolutionary theory. As social animals, humans need to make very quick judgments about potential threats with people that we're interacting with. So fast processing of heavily masculine features, that are commonly associated with aggression, would lead to a judgment that someone is a risk and should not be trusted. Imagine a time earlier in our evolutionary history when we had a fraction of a second to decide whether someone who jumped out at us is a risk. The man with more feminine features may be far less likely to hurt us, and we carry this evolutionary history with us even today.

If you are taking this course to help you become more influential, some of these studies can be depressing. It's hard to change fundamental elements of your appearance, such as the bone structure of your face. But you can do a few little things to look more attractive. Most important, groom your hair and skin so that they're neat, and smile a lot. Both neatness and smiling are associated with attractiveness and will help you get perceived as positive in other ways. Of course, how you look isn't all that matters. There are certainly examples of average looking, or even below-average looking, leaders who win over a company full, or even a country full, of people. What have these agents done over time to build credibility and trust with their targets of influence?

First, they have ability, skills, and competencies that allow them to do things effectively. In other words, trustworthy people are competent. Second, trustworthy people have benevolence; they intend to help you. Another way to say this is that they are caring. Third, they have integrity; they abide by a set of principles that is clear and sensible. That's another way of saying that trustworthy people are consistent in how they behave. So if you want to be seen as trustworthy, to lay the groundwork for future success as an agent of influence, then you should practice three Cs. You should strive to be competent, caring, and consistent.

This model allows us to move beyond initial impressions and offers specific suggestions about what you can do to develop a reputation for trustworthiness. Any agent who wishes to influence other people can work to correct misperceptions that occur as a result of facial features or other factors outside the agent's control. For example, imagine the day you start a new job. Your boss comes up and says, "You look a lot like my ex-husband. It really bothers me." For reasons that have nothing to do with you, you're starting off in a hole, or to use a budgeting analogy, you're starting off with a trust deficit that may make it hard to influence. Your best bet is to develop trust by remembering the three Cs. Work hard to build knowledge, and be competent in your work. Look after your boss' interests, and be caring. And demonstrate concern for fairness, being consistent in how you make decisions. If you pursue these vigorously, you can increase your trustworthiness and the chance that your boss will trust you and maybe give you a promotion in the future. In other words, by building your trustworthiness, you create greater opportunity to wield influence successfully in your work place.

So far, we've discussed how looks and behavior can influence how you are perceived, including whether people will trust you. But I've left out an important characteristic. Imagine your favorite sports team, and picture someone you've never met wearing that team's cap or jersey. What do you think about that person? Probably a pretty nice person, smart, sociable, certainly has good judgment. It's funny how the mere label of "we're on the same team" can influence judgments. There's a long history of research in social psychology about the powerful effect that being placed on the same team can have on us.

One of the most famous of these experiments will sound like it came straight out of William Golding's 1954 novel, *Lord of the Flies*. Muzafer Sherif, when he was on faculty at the University of Oklahoma, took 22 boys, age 11 and 12, to a summer camp at Robbers Cave State Park in Oklahoma. The boys were split into two camps, the Rattlers and the Eagles, and over two weeks went through three phases of an experiment. In the first phase of the experiment, lasting just under a week, the teams worked independently, and the relationship among the boys was developed and studied. In the second phase, the groups were introduced to each other and asked to compete in a series of contests that included baseball, tug of war, and touch football. In the third phase, the groups were brought together and given tasks that they had to collaborate on to achieve.

What happened? Just as in *Lord of the Flies*, things got a little crazy in the second phase. A variety of conflicts emerged between the two groups. At one point the Eagles stole and burned the Rattlers' flag, and each team raided the other's cabins, messing up beds, throwing around personal items, and even cutting canoes adrift. As relationships became even more tense, the groups stopped wanting to have anything to do with each other. And they would yell and curse at the others whenever they were in sight. The experimenters' reports indicate that on multiple occasions the boys had to be separated from each other, including a food fight where rolls and mashed potatoes became weapons. After the contests were over, the boys were asked to rate characteristics of the members of each group. They rated members of their own group favorably—were brave and friendly. And the other group, those members were rated unfavorably—they're sneaky and stinkers.

Fortunately, the third phase of Sherif's experiment showed that people can overcome intergroup hostility and can cooperate with so-called outsiders. Let's focus for a minute on the power of group identification. In the Robbers Cave experiment, there was a prolonged process in which groups formed, got to know each other, and then competed with another similarly cohesive group. This situation does happen, particularly in sports, but it happens less often when people are working together in the same organization or going to classes in the same school. In these settings there typically isn't overt competition between groups. So let's ask, does the general process of bias toward the in-group and against the out-group also occur in other settings? Or, worded in terms of influence, is someone on your own team more likely to be trusted and listened to than someone on the other team? The answer is a definitive yes. And this is where the work of another famous social psychologist, Henri Tajfel, comes into play.

Tajfel and his colleagues were interested in whether more neutral situations might lead to the same kinds of intergroup conflict. So rather than inducing competition, as Sherif had done, Tajfel would simply group people together arbitrarily. In some experiments he grouped them according to whether they over or under estimated the number of dots flashed on a screen. In another study, he grouped people based on whether they preferred paintings by Klee or Kandinsky. At the extreme, Tajfel and one of his colleagues, Michael Billig, grouped people by flip of a coin—heads you're over there, tails you're over here. To think that people would treat others differently based on groupings created by a coin flip sounds crazy, but that's exactly what happened. Participants in Tajfel's studies described members of their own group more favorably than members of the other group, and they were more generous to members of their own group, as compared to members of the other group.

How does this relate to influence? What this suggests is that mere sense of shared group membership can increase liking and trust. So the agents who are most influential are those that have some overlap in group membership with their targets. This plays out in the real world. Consider what every athlete, athletic coach, or university president does upon being selected by a new team. He puts on the proper uniform. Think back to the last press conference you saw with a new team member, whether it was a basketball player drafted or a university president hired, for that new team member almost certainly wore a jersey, a hat or a tie of the new team. This was the case when football coach Rich Rodriguez was hired from West Virginia to coach the Michigan Wolverines. He was wearing the right tie, all maize and blue, but Rodriguez's story shows that there's a bit more to successful influence than wearing the right clothes; you have to talk the talk as well. At his opening press conference, he didn't do a very good job convincing others he was part of the team. When he was asked by a reporter, "do you have to be a Michigan man to be the Michigan coach?" Rodriguez replied, "gosh, I hope not. They hired me."

In the book *Three and Out*, author John Bacon describes Rodriguez's troubled three years at University of Michigan. The scene was described as the start of a rocky relationship with some of the school's big athletic donors. You see, a Michigan man is an idea that people in Ann Arbor talk about, an idea about being someone with pride, and courage, and a love for the team. Not all of the former Michigan coaches had played at Michigan, so being a Michigan man wasn't really just about where you went to school. If Rodriguez had done a little more research and learned some about the team and the meaning of this phrase, he might have answered the question differently. A much better answer to this question, one that would have put Rodriguez squarely on the team and helped him through some of those difficult times would have been, you don't have to have played here at Michigan to coach here. Some of the best Michigan coaches didn't play at Michigan, but like each of them, I will strive to live up to the ideals of being a Michigan man. I'm honored by the opportunity to be part of that tradition of excellence. Research by Sherif, Tajfel, and others, and the story of Rich Rodriguez, suggest that shared group membership matters. And agents who carefully manage perception that they are part of the team will be much better able to influence. Wearing the right clothing helps, but saying the right things makes a difference too.

Let's move to another agent characteristic that can have a huge impact on the success or failure of an influence attempt—charisma. Charisma, which focuses even more on saying the right things in the right way, is often considered a magic quality of leadership that arouses loyalty and enthusiasm. And if you think of it as a rare and magical quality, you might also think that we're back to facial features and other immutable characteristics of agents. There is actually a growing body of evidence suggesting that with training, anyone can become more charismatic. A study by John Antonakis, Marika Fenley, and Sue Liechti, all from the University of Lausanne, compared managers who received charisma training to those who did not. While the groups were similar before training, the trained groups showed higher levels of charisma after training according to their colleagues back at work, so the training worked, but what exactly did it include?

One of the authors hosted a five-hour training session with lots of discussion and practice. In addition, trainees were given feedback about the ways in which they were and were not charismatic. They were also given tips on charismatic speaking, which involves using metaphors and stories, setting high expectations, and having confidence. Charismatic speakers demonstrate passion with gestures and animated voice tone. We will actually discuss these ideas again in a later lecture, but for our purposes here, you should know that learners were given feedback and opportunities to practice both verbal and nonverbal behaviors, and as a result, they became more charismatic leaders at work. So charisma really isn't some magical, inborn ability. It's something that anyone can develop with feedback and targeted practice.

Certainly not all of us have the time and resources to get hours of training and coaching that participants in the Antonakis study received. but not all is lost. Olivia Fox Cabane, a consultant and frequent trainer on the topic of charisma, published a book called *The Charisma Myth*. In the book, she offers plenty of helpful advice that anyone can learn from. For example, Cabane notes that people who are judged as charismatic are typically confident and passionate and convey this through posture, gestures, and vocal tones. She argues that the path forward for all of us is clear: don't try to act; just make yourself confident and passionate. But how do we do that?

According to Cabane, charisma begins in the mind. And what your mind believes, your body manifests. As a result, she offers a series of exercises to help people become more confident. Much of that begins with ridding yourself of physical and psychological discomfort. To deal with physical discomfort, which can make you fidget and look anxious, Cabane argues that you should prevent it when possible. But, when discomfort does occur, you need to recognize and remedy it right away. This suggests if you are uncomfortable, you should act on it rather than assume that people won't notice. Charismatic people take charge of situations, and then they change those situations so that they appear confident.

Suppose, for example, you're starting a new sales job, and you're meeting a potential customer in an informal setting, the local coffee shop. When you arrive at the coffee shop, you're wearing your heavy coat. It's initially cold when you sit, so you leave it on, but over time you become quite uncomfortable. While waiting, being polite, for a good break in the conversation, your discomfort is probably already showing. And your discomfort undermines your ability to appear confident and connect with the person you're talking to. You will be more comfortable and seem more competent if you apologetically interrupt and say, Oh, I'm sorry. Do you mind if I take off my coat? It feels hot in here.

The same idea should apply when you are cold, when your mouth is dry, or when the sun is in your eyes. If you take charge and do something to reduce your discomfort, you'll prevent inadvertently giving off a series of nonverbal cues that undermine any sense that you're charismatic. If you can prevent the appearance of nervousness, lack of confidence, and discomfort, then your potential customer sitting in that coffee shop will listen more carefully and be more likely to buy.

For psychological discomfort, Cabane suggests an exercise called responsibility transfer. It's a simple process that you can follow when you begin to get anxious. It asks you to, first, sit comfortably and relaxed; second, take a deep breath, and then pick an entity, God, fate, a loved one, whatever fits you, and imagine in your mind that benevolent, caring presence. Now, finally, imagine lifting the weight of everything you're anxious about and placing it in the hands of that entity. Let's return to the coffee shop where you're meeting your new customer. What happens if a group of friends bumps into you during this meeting? If you're like me, you might be nervous making introductions around a big group. Your discomfort might be misinterpreted by your customer as, "boy, these people aren't important," or, "I'm nervous to be seen here with you in this conversation." These misinterpretations of your inner state can seriously undermine your ability to make a favorable impression and close any subsequent deal. If you gather your thoughts for a minute, take a deep breath and do a responsibility transfer, then you will be more ready to make introductions so that there are no misunderstandings.

While talking about agent characteristics that benefit influence, it's easy to walk away thinking some people are born lucky; they're likeable, attractive, or have trustworthy facial features. But as Cabane suggests in her book, there are quite a few things that you can do to maximize your chances of being an influential agent. Let me offer two more specific suggestions from her book that will help you be perceived as charismatic, and thus be more likely to influence the person you're talking to. First, the next time you meet someone new, make sure you're both comfortable. Get the setting right so you can focus your attention on getting to know the person rather than worrying about being too hot, or too cold, or having to go to the bathroom. Second, you can try one of Cabane's training tools summarized in her book to improve your nonverbal behaviors. She suggests adopting the body language of someone who's depressed, slumping your shoulders and hanging your head. Then, keeping that position, try to imagine being excited. You'll find it quite difficult. Now do the opposite; put a smile on your face, and raise your arms in the air as if you won the big game or the big jackpot. Stay in that position and try, just try, to feel depressed. Doing this exercise a few times may help remind you of how the mind reads the body and allows it to guide mood. So the use of a smile and great posture can actually help you feel more confident, and you could do that before heading into a meeting. If you do this, it may really give you that extra boost that will help you be persuasive.

In this lecture, we've talked about beauty, trustworthiness, shared group membership, and charisma. I opened the lecture by saying you might get lured into a conversation with someone doing a door-to-door survey. How could that happen? Imagine that the person standing there is attractive with a face you cannot help but think, this is a truly nice person. And guess what? She's wearing your favorite team's jersey as well. These are the kind of subtle cues that can influence your decision. If you aren't careful, you might just get roped into answering that survey while your dinner gets cold.

What we've discussed in this lecture are all positive characteristics of agents, but there is a dark side to influence, as we all know. What leads some people to use tools of influence to cheat other people? We'll explore that question in our next lecture.

The Dark Side of Influence
Lecture 3

In our last lecture, we discussed the positive characteristics of agents that helped them to be persuasive. In this lecture, we'll delve into the negative characteristics that lead people to use persuasion to exploit others. We'll explore the characteristics of con artists and learn the differences between con artists and people who are skilled, ethical persuaders. Research has confirmed what is now being called a "dark triad" of personality characteristics, and people with these characteristics are more likely to lie, cheat, and steal from others. In the context of influence, these types of people are more likely to have harmful motives and use deceitful methods. Clearly, it is helpful to know more about such people to avoid their tricks.

Bernie Madoff's Ponzi Scheme

- On June 29, 2009, Bernie Madoff, head of a well-known investment firm, was sentenced to 150 years in prison for running one of the biggest financial frauds in U.S. history. Madoff was operating what's known as a Ponzi scheme. The scheme is named for Charles Ponzi, who attracted investors in the 1920s with a promised high rate of return and propped up the lie by paying his earliest investors with money from new investors. The scheme worked until Ponzi ran out of new investors.

- In his version of the Ponzi scheme, Madoff falsified investment records to show dramatic returns. In actuality, he was paying early investors with new investment money and spending some of the original deposits to fund an extravagant lifestyle.
  - At the time of his indictment, Madoff had an investment portfolio that his records showed was worth $64.8 billion.

  - But according to the trustee appointed to liquidate the accounts and pay back investors, the amount of money invested in Madoff's fund was only $36 billion. On top of that, about half of what had gone into the fund was missing.

- Madoff's personality seemed to combine charm and influence with a callous disregard for others. Among many different types of personality characteristics, three are central to this type of behavior: Machiavellianism, narcissism, and psychopathy. Researchers refer to these as the "dark triad" of personality.

Machiavellianism

- Machiavellianism is named, of course, for the Italian philosopher Niccolo Machiavelli. Individuals who score high in Machiavellianism on personality tests tend to be those who manipulate others for their own gain.

- A team of European researchers designed an interesting experiment that captures Machiavellianism in action.
  - o Participants in this experiment were given an opportunity to play a game in which they alternated between playing with a computer and with a person. In both conditions, players decided how much money from a designated pot they would share with their human or electronic partners.

  - o If the partners thought the amount of money offered to them wasn't fair, they could choose to punish the players by reducing how much money they got to keep. In other words, partners could take revenge if they thought that the players were being stingy. Of course, the computer did not make judgments about the players' stinginess.

  - o Players who scored higher in Machiavellianism withheld more money in trials with the computer and gave away just enough when they played with human partners to avoid being punished. Added up across all trials, higher Machiavellians earned the most.

  - o Just as interesting in this study were imaging results for the brains of participants. MRI results indicated that those high in Machiavellianism had significant brain activity in a brain region associated with concerns for punishment. Machiavellians are highly sensitive to punishment; thus, in the experiment, they acted with restraint when punishment was a factor, but when punishment was not possible, they kept all the money they could.

- Peter Jonason and Gregory Webster, two scholars who have studied the dark triad extensively, sought to boil down all measures of Machiavellianism, narcissism, and psychopathy into a short, easily-administered survey. They settled on 12 simple statements that scale people from low to high along these dimensions. Two of the statements used to measure Machiavellianism are: "I tend to manipulate others to get my way" and "I have used deceit or lied to get my way."

Narcissism

- Narcissists are those who are profoundly self-centered, a trait that leads to extravagantly self-serving behavior.

- One measure of narcissism used in management studies is the number of times an executive uses the first person in speeches. In quotes from an interview with Barbara Walters, Madoff used "I" frequently and tried to present a positive picture of his crimes.

- In their dark triad survey, Jonason and Webster use the following statements to measure narcissism: "I tend to want others to admire me" and "I tend to want others to pay attention to me."

Psychopathy

- When we hear the word "psychopath," we often imagine a serial killer, but the reality is far less dramatic. Many people who display signs of psychopathy are not violent, and very few commit violent crimes. The more accurate depiction of the psychopath is the rare individual who is not concerned with the feelings or welfare of others. This lack of empathy and sensitivity means that these individuals have fewer constraints on their behavior; thus, they are more likely to inflict pain or damage on others.

- This trait has been studied in detail by Robert Hare, who developed a clinical checklist that is commonly used to diagnosis psychopathy.

- In a 2011 book about Hare's checklist called *The Psychopath Test*, author Jon Ronson describes his meeting with Al Dunlap, the former CEO of Sunbeam. Ronson was interested in exploring whether Dunlap met the criteria of a psychopathic personality.
  - Dunlap fit many of the characteristics on Hare's checklist but not all of them; further, Dunlap himself claimed that he feels sadness and remorse.

  - According to Ronson's description, however, Dunlap continues to feel justified for making ruthless and sometimes unethical decisions in the context of helping Sunbeam return to profitability.

  - In the end, Sunbeam went bankrupt because of the questionable business and accounting practices that Dunlap supported. As with Madoff, the primary beneficiary of Dunlap's activities was Dunlap himself.

- Jonason and Webster's statements to measure psychopathy are: "I tend to lack remorse" and "I tend to be callous or insensitive."

The Dark Triad in Males versus Females
- Is it the case that only men exhibit the dark triad characteristics or engage in the types of influence attempts—deceitful and manipulative—that the dark triad engenders?

- In a 2012 study, authors Peter Jonason, Sarah Slomski, and Jamie Partyka found that people who score high in narcissism and Machiavellianism tend to use hard influence tactics—those that involve demands or threats. In contrast, soft tactics involve appeals to logic or emotion.

- Jonason and his colleagues also found that men use hard tactics more often than women and that more men than women score high in the dark triad traits.

"The Toxic Triangle"

- In a 2007 paper entitled "The Toxic Triangle," authors Art Padilla, Robert Hogan, and Robert Kaiser use the term "destructive leadership" to explain what happens in a situation with a poisonous combination of agent, target, and context.

Individuals who score high on dark triad traits are more likely than others to employ deception, lies, and trickery in their influence attempts.

© George Doyle/Stockbyte.

- The paper uses Fidel Castro as an example. Castro did some positive things for Cuba, but he also engaged in campaigns to imprison and kill those who opposed him. Even at a young age, Castro was seen as idealistic, bold, and skilled at self-promotion. He also came to hate the United States and what it stood for. In this way, Castro fulfills the quintessential agent profile for a destructive leader—a narcissistic agent who espouses an ideology of hate.

- How could such a leader acquire and maintain power? At the time of the Cuban communist revolution, many Cuban citizens were ready for a charismatic leader promising power to the people. The troubled economic and political atmosphere at the time, marked by intense poverty and corruption, made a strong leader like Castro far more compelling. Many of the people who stood to lose the most—members of the middle class—fled the country, increasing the relative number of supportive followers of Castro. Thus, both the target and the context were conducive to Castro's emergence as a powerful leader.

- Although it is not clear whether Castro's rise could have been avoided, it is useful to consider that certain targets of influence and certain contexts favor bold, risk-taking, and potentially destructive leaders. Awareness of this fact may be useful in helping opponents rally support against such leaders, preventing them from using influence tactics to gain too much power.

A Question of Ethics
- The ethicality of any influence attempt can be viewed along a continuum. Most people would agree that a politician who uses his or her likeability to influence voters to endorse a traffic intersection redesign that saves lives is "good." Most would also agree that someone who uses blatant lies drawn from a Machiavellian desire to cheat others out of money is "bad." But what about the sales pitch that involves no overt lie, just an omission of some detail to help structure the most compelling argument?

- There seems to be a line between the effective, ethical persuader and the con man.
  - The con man's influence efforts are characterized by malice and misinformation. These characteristics capture both motive (a desire to win at another's expense) and method (outcome pursued at any cost).

  - In contrast, the ethical persuader has both a socially beneficial motive and an ethical approach that involves accurate information. Some of the tools used by this persuader may be similar to those of the con man, but the difference in motive and the willingness to use accurate information make the influence attempt ethical.

- Another difference between an ethical persuader and a con artist is perspective. Con artists focus on the here and now and will use any tactic at their disposal to get their way immediately. Ethical persuaders take the long view. They work to develop trusting relationships that set the stage for later influence.

Application: Practicing Skepticism

- How can you avoid becoming a victim of agents who have narcissistic, Machiavellian, and psychopathic personality traits? We all know not to believe someone who offers us something that is too good to be true. Put your skepticism to practice by looking for suspicious claims in newspapers, on television, and on the Internet.

- You should also adopt the advice of a Russian proverb: Trust but verify. If someone you don't know tries to gain your confidence, double-check that person's story. If you receive a suspicious e-mail, don't click on its links. Instead, do an online search to see if others have reported that e-mail as a fraud. When dealing with your investment advisor, ask for records of your transactions and a full explanation of both your gains and losses.

Suggested Reading

Henriques, *The Wizard of Lies*.

Ronson, *The Psychopath Test*.

Activities to Try

1. Look for suspicious claims in newspapers, on television, and on websites. What is it about the claims that makes them dubious?

2. The next time someone you don't know tries to gain your confidence, adopt the advice contained in a Russian proverb: Trust but verify. Double-check the agent's story. For example, you might check e-mails from an unknown source by doing an online search to see if others have reported that source as fraudulent.

The Dark Side of Influence
Lecture 3—Transcript

In the aftermath of a terrible storm, there is eerie quiet. I drove through a small town that had been hit by a tornado less than an hour before. The roof was completely off one farmhouse, and what looked to have been a barn was a pile of timber and hay. Crises, like a tornado, hurricanes Andrew, Katrina, or Sandy, or the Midwest floods of 1993 and 2008, bring out the best and sometimes the worst in people. To be more precise for our lecture today, crises sometimes bring out the worst people. In the eerie quiet after a crisis, what type of influence agent will emerge to offer his aid? Following a series of storms on the East Coast in 2011, Dominik Sadowski and his employees from Precision Builders, a Camden, New Jersey firm, would visit neighbors and knock on doors. They'd go into homes and offer to do free inspections and explained that anything they did would be covered by insurance.

Sadowski sold his services by presenting himself as a hero, there to save the day. The real truth was that Sadowski and his crew were criminals. In some cases they would inspect homes that were undamaged and actually create damage with their tools. This is why Sadowski was convicted of fraud and sentenced to four years probation and 100 hours of community service. In other similar cases, contractors offer great deals, take deposit money, and then disappear, never to return. Following hurricanes Rita and Katrina, researchers at Louisiana State University estimated that over 9,000 households were subject to some type of contractor fraud. Contractors like Sadowski are using a very old bag of tricks that we often label "the con game." Con games, or confidence games, involve a simple sequence of gaining someone's confidence and then exploiting it for personal gain. The con is deeply ingrained in popular culture with movies like *The Music Man*, written by Iowa's very own Meredith Willson, starring Robert Preston; *The Sting*, starring Newman and Redford; *Dirty Rotten Scoundrels*, with Steve Martin and Michael Caine; and *Catch Me If You Can* with Leonardio DiCaprio. Each movie captures the exploits of a charming criminal or two who get their way with smiles and lies.

We have a love-hate relationship with con artists. It's hard not to like the characters played by Preston and DiCaprio. They're protagonists of these movies, aren't they? But in real life, con artists are not heroes. There's something about them that has led them to refine and improve their influence skills and then use them to take advantage of other people. In our last lecture, we talked about the positive characteristics of agents that help them to be persuasive. In this lecture, we'll delve into negative characteristics that lead people to use persuasion to exploit others. We're going to explore what makes someone a con artist and how such a person is different than a skilled ethical persuader.

Before we go further let me preview the key takeaway. Research has confirmed what is now being called the dark triad of personality characteristics, and people with these characteristics are more likely to lie, cheat and steal from others. In the context of influence, these particular types of people are more likely to have harmful motives and use deceitful methods. Clearly, it's helpful to know more about such people so you don't get lied to, cheated on, and stolen from. But before we talk about the dark triad, I want to tell you another story.

In November 2008, Bernie Madoff was on top of the world. Head of a family-run investment business, Bernard L. Madoff Investment Securities, LLC, he had clients all over the world, including movie stars like Kyra Sedgwick, Kevin Bacon, former talk show host Larry King, and even former baseball great Sandy Koufax. His firm had pioneered the use of software for stock trading. He later served on the NASDAQ board of governors and served on the board of directors for the Securities Industry Association. This was a man who'd been at the center of Wall Street for decades. But on June 29, 2009, Madoff was sentenced to 150 years in prison for running what has become one of the biggest financial frauds in U.S. History. What did Madoff do? And, how did he do it? And perhaps, most relevant for our purposes in this lecture, why did he do it?

It turns out that Madoff was running what has become known as a Ponzi scheme. The scheme is named for a gentleman, Charles Ponzi, who in the 1920s attracted investors with a promised high rate of return, 50 percent, and propped up that lie by paying his earliest investors with money from the new investors. His scheme worked up until Ponzi ran out of new investors. In his version of the Ponzi scheme, Bernie Madoff falsified investment records so they indicated dramatic returns. In actuality, he was doing what Ponzi did, paying old investors with new investors' money, spending original deposits to fund an extravagant personal lifestyle. At the time of his indictment, Madoff had an investment portfolio that, on paper, and in his account statements to those investors, said was worth $64.8 billion. To put this in perspective, this is larger than the gross domestic product of quite a few countries, a bit less than Ecuador, but more than Luxembourg, for example. So on paper, Madoff was running a small country.

But how much real money was in the accounts? According to Irving Picard, the trustee appointed by the court to liquidate the accounts and pay back investors whatever he could, the amount of money invested in Madoff's fund was $36 billion, only a little more than half of what the records said. So as a start, Madoff lied to many people about how much money they actually had in their investment accounts. On top of that, about half of what actually went into the fund was simply gone. That's $18 billion spent on houses, apartments, boats, art, and some other things that Picard could not even trace.

Who did Madoff lie to? Whose money did he spend? *New York Magazine* profiled the victims, and they included famous people, like Steven Spielberg and Kevin Bacon. But the list also included regular people who lost their entire life savings. Phyllis Molchatsky, for example, worked a long career as a manager and put away money whenever she could, eventually putting it all into the fund run by Madoff. On paper, as she neared retirement, she had $3.8 million. Once the scandal broke, she had nothing. Her whole life savings was gone.

Madoff is a great example of someone with a personality that combines charm and influence with a callous disregard for others. Among many different types of personality characteristics, there are three that are particularly central to this type of behavior: Machiavellianism, narcissism, and psychopathy. Researchers refer to these as the dark triad of personality. Each of these three personality traits is somewhat distinct, and as I will note, research suggests that each can lead some people to do harm with their use of influence.

Let's first look at Machiavellianism, which is named for the Italian Philosopher, Niccolo Machiavelli. Individuals who score high in Machiavellianism tend to be the kind who manipulate others for their own gain. A team of European researchers designed an interesting experiment that captures Machiavellianism in action. Participants in this experiment were given an opportunity to play a game where they rotated between playing against a computer and playing against a person. In both conditions, participants decided how much money from a designated pot they would share with their partner, again, either a person or computer. If the partner thought the amount of money offered them wasn't fair, the game was structured so that they could choose to punish the participants and reduce how much money they got to keep. In other words, the partner was given leeway to take revenge if she became angry with how stingy the research participant was being.

Of course, when the playing partner was a computer, it would take whatever money was given gladly and not hold a grudge. Computers are convenient like that. But when the partner was a person, well, that was another story. How do you win at this game? Who gets the most money? Well, the people who earn the most in this game are those who pay just enough to human partners on rounds where the human partner is playing, and they quickly switch strategy to paying as little as possible when the computer is playing. It takes a little thought and strategizing to win big in this game, and can you guess who did best? People higher in Machiavellian personality withheld more money in the trials with the computer and gave just enough when they were playing against people to avoid being punished. Adding up across all trials, higher Machiavellians earned the most. They figured out the system, were ruthless when it worked against that unfeeling computer, but played nice when it was necessary against the person who could punish them.

Just as interesting in this particular study were imaging results from the brains of participants. These participants actually played while they were in an MRI machine. The MRI results, the pictures of their brains, indicate that those high in Machiavellianism had significant brain activity in our brain region associated with concern for punishment. Machiavellians are highly sensitive to punishment, so in the experiment, they acted with smart restraint when punishment was a factor, but when punishment was not, they were working.

Their brain activity was going. They kept all they could. Think about it this way. Keep an eye on someone like this, and they'll play nice. Turn your back, and who knows what they might do in pursuit of their own self-interest. Now that I describe it that way, I realize I live with a Machiavellian personality. Lola is the best behaved dog when she knows you're watching. But turn your back, she's on the table eating a Thanksgiving turkey, probably should have called her Mach.

Peter Jonason and Gregory Webster, two scholars who've studied the dark triad extensively, sought to boil down all measures of Machiavellianism, narcissism, and psychopathy into a short, easily-administered survey. They settled, after much research, on 12 simple statements that allow us to scale people from low to high along these dimensions. Here are two of the statements that they use to measure Machiavellianism: I tend to manipulate others to get my way; I have used deceit or lied to get my way.

Moving to the second of the dark triad characteristics, we come to narcissism. This personality trait means that someone is profoundly self-centered, which leads to extravagantly self-serving behavior. Rather than talk about a research study for narcissism, I'd like to return to Bernie Madoff. Last we left him, he was sitting in a federal penitentiary, and in an interview with Barbara Walters, he was asked what he thinks about all this negative publicity he received. Does he understand why? And does he regret what he has done? "I understand why clients hate me. The gravy train is over," he said. "I can live with that." He went on, "The average person thinks I robbed widows and orphans," he added. "I made wealthy people wealthier." Notice the pattern of quotes here. Despite his outright lies overall, he excuses it and frames what he did positively. He helped people.

One measure of narcissism used in management studies is the number of times an executive uses the first person in speeches. In these quotes from the Walters interview, Madoff uses I frequently. And he also tries to present what he did, the lying, the cheating, the stealing, somehow in a positive light. Remember the truth, though. Madoff only made money for people who were smart enough to withdraw their money in time. In other words, if they were Machiavellian and didn't trust him, they probably made money with him.

But then, Madoff left many people holding nothing. So who benefited from this gravy train that Madoff created? Bernie Madoff, of course.

The use of I and unconditional positive self-regard of narcissists overall reminds me of another business leader, Donald Trump. Trump likes to be the center of attention and finds many ways to make that happen, even if they have nothing at all to do with his business dealings. Perhaps most obvious is his habit of naming things after himself. On the first floor of Trump Tower in New York there's a breakfast place called Trump Café. When Trump opened Trump International Hotel and Tower in Chicago, he made sure there was an outstanding outdoor bar. Its name? The Terrace at Trump. While you're there, if you visit, make sure to use your Trump Card so you can earn points toward further Trump Attaché services. Jonason and Webster, who built that dark triad survey, used the following two statements to measure narcissism: I tend to want others to admire me. I tend to want others to pay attention to me.

The third and final of the dark triad characteristics is psychopathy. Psychopathy is present when someone has little concern for others and their welfare. When we hear this word, though, we often imagine a serial killer, knife in hand, sneaking up on an unsuspecting victim. The reality is far less dramatic. Most people who display signs of psychopathy are not violent and very few ever commit violent crime. The more accurate depiction of the psychopath is the rare individual who's not particularly concerned about the feelings or welfare of others. This lack of empathy means that those individuals have fewer constraints on their behavior, so they're more likely to end up doing mean or hurtful things.

This particular trait has been studied in detail by Professor Robert Hare, who developed a clinical checklist that's commonly used to diagnose psychopathy. I should note, by the way, that the term psychopathy is not recognized by psychiatrists, who prefer the term antisocial personality disorder. But, in social and organizational psychology, the term psychopathy is very much a part of the research vocabulary. While we're clearing up details I should note that Hare conceptualizes psychopathy to include narcissism, but this is really a matter of how one prefers to slice the pie of dysfunctional personalities. More often when someone displays one, they display the others, the whole pie, as well.

In a 2011 book about Hare's checklist, called *The Psychopath Test*, author Jon Ronson describes his journey to Florida, where he meets Al Dunlap, the former CEO of Sunbeam. Ronson was interested to explore whether Dunlap met the criteria on Hare's checklist of a psychopathic personality. Upon arriving at the home, Ronson looked around, and he noted that Dunlap had a particular theme to his decorating. Dunlap's home was adorned with statues and paintings of lions, and eagles, and all types of predators. In an interview with Ronson, Dunlap explains that he believes in carnivores. His record at Sunbeam, which involved a series of ruthless decisions to fire people, leading to the nickname "Chainsaw Al," seems to support the idea that he likes carnivores. Dunlap, for the record, also engaged in shady accounting practices that artificially boosted Sunbeam's stock price.

Although Dunlap fit many of the characteristics on Hare's checklist, he didn't fit all of them, and he certainly denies being a psychopath, because, he says, he does feel sadness and remorse, such as when his dog died when he was a kid. Although, if you listen carefully to his interview, as described by Ronson, it's easy to wonder just how much remorse he feels. Certainly Dunlap continues to feel justified in making ruthless and sometimes unethical decisions in the context of helping Sunbeam return to profitability. In the end, however, Sunbeam ended up in bankruptcy because of the questionable business and accounting practices that Dunlap supported. So as with Bernie Madoff, the primary beneficiary of Dunlap's behavior was Dunlap himself, or those lucky individuals who did not trust him and sold all their stock before the truth came to light. Peter Jonason and Gregory Webster's statements to measure psychopathy are: I tend to lack remorse, and I tend to be callous or insensitive. In Al Dunlap we actually see all of the quintessential elements of the dark triad, a desire to win at all cost—Machiavellianism; high self-regard—narcissism; and a disregard for others—psychopathy.

The dark triad offers insights into the question about the differences between ethical and unethical use of persuasion. Individuals high on dark triad traits are much more likely than anyone else to employ deception, lies, and trickery in their attempts to influence. As I said before, being aware that there are people like this can help us avoid being the next victim of theft or fraud.

While discussing the dark triad, you probably notice that the examples so far have all been men. Is it the case that only men exhibit these characteristics and that only men engage in the types of influence attempts, deceitful and manipulative, that the dark triad engenders? To find out, let's turn to a 2012 study authored by Peter Jonason, Sarah Slomski, and Jamie Partyka. Not surprisingly, this study found that people high in narcissism and Machiavellianism tend to more frequently use hard influence tactics, those tactics that involve demands and threats to get what you want. In contrast, soft tactics involve using appeals to logic or emotion. We'll discuss these in more detail in a subsequent lecture. Jonason and his colleagues also found that men use more hard tactics than women. Why is that the case? Well, they found that more men than women were high in the dark triad traits. So the answer to the question, do only men exhibit these traits, is no, but there are certainly more men than women who fit the scary dark triad profile, and they're more likely to use hard tactics.

So far we've been discussing the dark triad in reference to the agent, the person who attempts to influence others. But when we look at the harmful ways that dark triad personalities can influence other people, it's important to look at the other components of our ATTiC framework as well. Do target, tactics and context also contribute to the success of a con? To answer that, let's turn to a 2007 paper entitled "The Toxic Triangle." In this paper, authors Art Padilla, Bob Hogan, and Robert Kaiser use the term destructive leadership to explain what happens when there's a poisonous combination of agent, target, and context. Professor Padilla and his colleagues use Fidel Castro as an example.

Castro did some positive things for Cuba, but in his time as the longest serving dictator in modern history, he also engaged in campaigns to imprison and kill those who opposed him. He was famous for long, rambling speeches that focused on himself more than the issues. Even at a young age, Castro was seen as idealistic, and bold, and quite skilled at self-promotion. He also came to hate the United States and everything it stood for. So here we have a narcissistic agent who espouses an ideology of hate; that's the quintessential agent profile for a destructive leader.

But how could such a leader come to and stay in power? The answer is in context. At the time of the Cuban communist revolution, many, although certainly not all citizens of Cuba, were ready for a charismatic leader promising reform and power to the people. The troubled economic and political atmosphere of the time marked by intense poverty and corruption made a strong leader, a strong principled leader, like Castro far more compelling than any alternative. Many of the people who stood to lose the most, the middle class, fled the country. So the relative number of supportive followers was increased. So both the targets and the context were conducive to Castro's emergence as a powerful leader.

While it is not at all clear whether historically Castro's rise could have been avoided, it's useful to consider that certain targets of influence and certain contexts favor bold, risk-taking and potentially destructive leaders. Awareness of this fact may be useful in helping opponents rally support against such leaders, preventing them from using influence tactics to gain too much power, which they will be likely to abuse.

As we wrap up this lecture it's worth reminding ourselves that the world is not often as black and white as we might like it to be. The dark triad exists along a continuum, as does the ethicality of any particular influence effort. Certainly we can agree that using your likeability to influence voters to endorse a traffic intersection redesign that saves lives is good, and surely we agree that using blatant lies drawn from a Machiavellian desire to cheat is bad. But what about the sales pitch that involves no overt lie, just an omission of some detail to help structure the most compelling argument and get the sale? I recently bought a piece of technology that has three features I like, and I actually told the sales rep about each of them and why I wanted them. The sales rep knew me, and he knew what other technology I owned. And he knew that one of those features would not work with my technology setup, but he failed to mention that fact. I learned it for myself less than an hour later. And here we enter the grey—between the black and white. The sales person's omission helped get that sale, but it had reduced my trust in him and in that store.

As we get further into the course, I'm not going to dig into the philosophical issues that would help us explore the boundaries between good and bad, but I will take a particular stance as it relates to influence and ethics. I believe there is a line between the effective ethical persuader and the con man. The con man's influence efforts are characterized by two things: malice and misinformation. This captures both motive—a desire to win at other's expense, and method—an outcome pursued at any cost. The ethical persuader will have both a socially beneficial motive and an ethical approach that involves accurate information. She will strive to accomplish goals that benefit more than just herself and do so in a way that is honest. Some of the tools that she uses may in other ways look the same as the con man, but the difference in motive and the willingness to use accurate information must be present for influence to be ethical. Another important difference between an ethical persuader and a con artist is their perspective. Con artists focus on the here and now, and they'll use any tactic at their disposal to get their way—right away. Ethical persuaders take the long view. They work to develop trusting relationships that set the stage for later influence.

In this lecture we've explored the dark side of influence. We've seen that agents who have narcissistic, Machiavellian, and psychopathic personality traits are likely to influence others in ways that involve lying, cheating, and stealing. But if we know these people are out there, how can we avoid becoming a victim? It's quite difficult to detect these people, because some of them can be very charming. But I will offer two tips. First, don't believe someone who offers you something that is too good to be true—money for nothing. A product substantially better than all of the competitors but somehow cheaper; a magical service that does absolutely everything you need, these are things you should be suspicious of. While I don't want you to be on the lookout and distrusting all the time, it is useful to practice skepticism. You can practice being a skeptic by looking for suspicious claims in newspapers, television, and websites. One common one is the claim by nutritional supplements to prevent disease. Most of these claims have not been independently verified by scientists, and the U.S. Food and Drug Administration does not heavily regulate, at least for now, ads for nutritional supplements. We all want to believe that a single, small pill, once a day, will prevent a heart attack or cure arthritis. But it's just not likely to be true, given the variety of factors that influence these health conditions. Talk to a few people and look for evidence elsewhere before buying.

The second thing you can try is this; adopt the advice contained in a Russian proverb: "Trust, but verify." In negotiations with the Soviet Union in the 1980s, Ronald Regan used this phrase frequently and publicly. It's also advice that is often followed by investigative reporters seeking to get to the bottom of a great story. I caution against overusing this as an approach to life, because it'll make you unhappy if you're thinking everyone's out to get you. But the next time someone you don't know tries to gain your confidence, maybe to get your money, double check the story. If it's an email, see if you can verify the source and the nature of the email from an independent source. Don't click on any links from any unsolicited emails. If you're interested because it sounds like a good deal, do an independent, online search to see if others have reported that email as a fraud. If it's your investment advisor sending you news, ask for specific transaction records and a full explanation of your gains, not just your losses. Can you verify the numbers you're being shown from a second source? When we hear what we want to hear it's easy to not be critical, but often, as in the case of Bernie Madoff's clients, that's exactly when we need to be.

In these last two lectures we've talked about agent characteristics, the positive and the negative. In the next lecture we'll move from agent to target and talk about the characteristics of targets that make them more susceptible to influence from both con artists and ethical persuaders.

Characteristics of Suggestible Targets
Lecture 4

In our last two lectures, we discussed characteristics of agents that made them more likely to be able to influence others. In this lecture, we shift to the target, examining the qualities that make people more likely to be influenced. Research indicates that some targets of influence are more suggestible than others. If you happen to be someone who has been called gullible, then knowledge and acceptance of this personal characteristic can help you escape becoming a victim of an influence expert with bad intentions.

Collectivism
- As we saw in an earlier lecture, experiments in social conformity show that some people are more likely to be concerned about and adhere to group norms. Such people are called collectivists. They value their connections with the group and will subsume individual preferences to the good of the group.

- Collectivism varies across individuals and cultures. Certain countries, such as Japan and Korea, have cultures that promote a high level of collectivism among their citizens. Countries with low levels of collectivism include the United States, Canada, and Australia.

- At these extremes, we observe differences in the way participants behave in social conformity experiments. Cultural collectivists are more likely to be influenced by others within a group to preserve harmony and consensus.

Suggestibility
- Another characteristic of targets that is relevant to persuasion is suggestibility. This term refers to a person's willingness to accept messages from the self or others. In effect, it is the likelihood that

something that is seen, heard, or felt will immediately be judged as true.

- One survey measure of suggestibility is the Multidimensional Iowa Suggestibility Scale (MISS). Created and owned by Professor Roman Kotov as part of his work as a doctoral student at the University of Iowa, MISS has dimensions that include consumer suggestibility, persuadability, peer conformity, and stubborn opinionatedness. These and other dimensions cover the various ways that information can come to people and potentially influence them—from the self, from peers, and from the media.

- Consumer suggestibility refers to how easily a person is persuaded by messages from the media about products and services. MISS statements related to this aspect of suggestibility include: "I often get information about products from commercials" and "After someone I know tries a new product, I will usually try it, too."

- Persuadability refers to how easily one is persuaded by information provided by peers. Those who strongly agree with the following statements have high scores on persuadability: "I can be convinced by a good argument" and "I get many good ideas from others."

- Peer conformity refers to how often someone conforms to the beliefs or activities of friends and colleagues in order to "fit in." Statements related to high peer conformity are: "My friends and I like the same things" and "I follow current fashion trends."

- As reported by Professor Kotov, the characteristic "stubborn opinionatedness" has a small but reliable negative correlation with other dimensions of suggestibility. Having higher levels of this characteristic renders someone less likely to be influenced by others. Statements related to this characteristic are: "I question what I see on the news" and "I have a strong opinion on most issues."

- Martin Brüne and colleagues from Ruhr University Bochum in Germany examined the relationship between suggestibility and acceptance of offers in an ultimatum game.
  - The ultimatum game is used in many decision-making studies and involves two players who interact to decide how they would share money given to them. In a typical sequence, one player is given some total of "money units." That player offers a percentage to a second player, who can either refuse or accept. If the second player accepts, both players keep the proposed sums, but if the second player refuses, neither player keeps any units.

  - As you might imagine, in the ultimatum game, a 50-50 split is considered fair, and everyone agrees to it. The interesting question is: What happens when the proposed split is not fair, say, 70-30? Is a player willing to refuse, even though it means that he or she won't get anything, just so the other player can't keep the unfair portion?

  - In Brüne's study, researchers found that in the most unfair situations—when a player was offered an 80-20 or 90-10 split—people with higher suggestibility were much more likely to acquiesce to the unfair proposal.

- Note that when an opportunity arises to influence someone and you are the agent, your chances of success depend not just on you but also on your target. If your target is more suggestible, then you are more likely to win even if what you're asking isn't fair. If your target is less suggestible, then you may not win even if you are a master at wielding influence.

Age

- Age is another important characteristic in determining how likely a target is to be influenced. Both younger and older adults are more susceptible to influence.

- Psychologists Laurence Steinberg and Kathryn Monahan, both from Temple University, examined people's resistance to peer influence. In this survey, participants were given pairs of opposing statements and asked to pick which statement described them better.

Older adults who are experiencing cognitive decline may become a target of choice for agents with bad intentions.

Examples of such statements included the following: "Some people go along with their friends just to keep their friends happy" versus "Other people refuse to go along with what their friends want to do, even though they know it will make their friends unhappy."

- o The researchers found that preteens and teens were less resistant to peer influence. The ability to resist influence increased gradually in the teen years until age 20, at which point, it appeared to level off.

- o Thus, it seems true that the preteen and early teen years are filled with concerns about fitting in with peers; this means that those in this age group are more likely to be influenced by peers, either for good or for bad.

- Natalie Denburg and colleagues at the University of Iowa and University of Southern California examined the question of susceptibility to influence in older adults.
  - o Denburg's work relies on what has been called the frontal lobe hypothesis of aging. This hypothesis suggests that as people age, changes occur in the prefrontal brain structures that undermine fundamental cognitive functions related to decision making. In some adults, these changes are disproportionately high.

o The results of Denburg's research suggest that older adults who are experiencing a natural decline in cognitive functioning are less likely to comprehend deceptive advertising and, thus, more likely to be influenced to make a purchase.

Motivation

- Motivation is a central element to the study of attitude change. Social psychologists have studied attitude change for some time, and a number of useful theories have emerged. One of these is called dual process theory. As advanced by professors Richard Petty and John Cacioppo, this theory suggests that attitudes can change through either central or peripheral routes.

  o Central routes are deliberate and effortful and occur when someone thinks carefully about a topic. The process here is one in which people collect information, deliberate on it, and then decide their attitudes toward the topic.

  o Peripheral routes occur outside of attention and awareness. Typically, people change their minds via peripheral routes when reminded of something positive (or negative) while thinking about the topic.

- A now-classic study examining central and peripheral processing was published in the *Journal of Consumer Research* in 1983. This study found that people's attitudes after viewing an advertisement could not be predicted solely by argument strength (a central route) or by whether a famous endorser was used (a peripheral route). Another factor to be considered was whether or not people were motivated to pay attention.

  o When people were made to believe that the information presented was personally relevant because they would be asked about it later, the strength of the arguments mattered. In this condition, having a famous endorser did not influence participants' attitudes toward the advertised product.

  o When people did not think the material was personally relevant because they were unlikely to have to do anything with the information later, the argument did not make a difference; attitudes were the same whether the arguments were strong or weak. But famous endorsers did make a difference!

o   In other words, when people aren't paying attention, peripheral cues, such as endorsers, are relevant. When people are paying attention, they pay enough attention to the argument that its quality matters.

o   Other studies have confirmed these findings. People are generally less likely to be influenced by extraneous factors if they are motivated to pay attention to the real arguments, the real features of the product, and so on. When targets are not motivated, they are more easily influenced by tactics that have little or nothing to do with the actual argument that is being used by the influencing agent.

•   The findings we've seen related to age and motivation are further supported by a 2011 review article by scholars Guang-Xin Xie and David Boush. Consistent with dual process theory, this review found that people who are either distracted or not motivated are more likely to be susceptible to false claims in ads. The authors also found support for age as an important factor. Memory deficits in older adults increase the likelihood that a deceptive ad will be believed.

Application: Fighting Susceptibility

•   In his book *Annals of Gullibility*, Stephen Greenspan offers four suggestions for fighting susceptibility: (1) Avoid acting impulsively, (2) design your own situations to avoid being pressured, (3) accept that you don't know everything, and (4) become more socially aware, paying careful attention to some of the characteristics and ploys of influence agents who have bad intentions.

•   To find out how suggestible you are, take the short online version of MISS available online (http://medicine.stonybrookmedicine. edu/psychiatry/faculty/kotov_r; scroll down to "Psychological instruments and manuals"). If you think you tend to be high in suggestibility, then be extra vigilant about overbuying or following friends into unwise activities.

- When you are about to make your next purchasing decision, step back and take some time to think. If an overbearing salesperson demands that you buy right away, ask yourself why that salesperson is in such a rush to close the sale. You might look for second opinions from someone who does not have a commission at stake or do some research in such sources as *Consumer Reports*.

Suggested Reading

Greenspan, *Annals of Gullibility*.

Petty and Cacioppo, *Communication and Persuasion*.

Activities to Try

1. Review the 21-item version of the Multidimensional Iowa Suggestibility Scale that is available online (http://medicine.stonybrookmedicine.edu/psychiatry/faculty/kotov_r; scroll down to "Psychological instruments and manuals"). Rate yourself to see your general level of suggestibility.

2. When you are about to make a significant decision, step back and take some extra time to think. Before you make a big purchase or a major decision, get second opinions from people who have no vested interest in your choice. If you see something advertised and it appeals to you, do research in such sources as *Consumer Reports* before buying.

Characteristics of Suggestible Targets
Lecture 4—Transcript

A powerful theme in literature is the deception of people who probably should have known better. In the Bible there's Eve being convinced that eating the fruit of the tree is in her best interests. In Virgil's *Aeneid*, the Trojans carry the gift of a wooden horse into their gates, thus sealing the fate of their impervious city by unwittingly bringing inside a group of Greek soldiers. In Shakespeare's *Othello*, a single misplaced handkerchief was all Othello needed to be convinced that his wife was unfaithful. And in Mark Twain's *The Adventures of Tom Sawyer*, the protagonist convinces Ben Rogers, Billy Fisher, Johnny Miller, and a string of other boys just how much fun it is to paint a fence, and he even lets them pay for the privilege to do it.

Many of us know people like Johnny Miller or Othello, people who are a bit too willing to believe. Does modern research support the idea that some people are more likely to be tricked or, for something less dramatic, convinced? The answer is an unequivocal yes. Returning to the ATTiC model created for this course, the first key refers to characteristics of the target being influenced. Research indicates that some targets of influence are more suggestible than others. If you happen to be someone who's been called gullible in the past, or maybe you know someone who has, then knowledge and acceptance of that personal characteristic can help you escape being a victim of an influence expert with bad intentions, like Bernie Madoff.

In our last lecture we discussed characteristics of agents that made them more likely to be able to influence. Now we're shifting to the target and examining what makes them more likely to be influenced. If you recall from the first lecture, Solomon Asch of Swarthmore College conducted a series of important experiments on social conformity. These experiments show that people who found themselves amidst others who claimed something obviously false—line A there, that's the one that matches—they would sometimes go along with the group and say out loud things they did not believe. But some of the subjects in these famous experiments would even come to believe something that their eyes weren't seeing. Videos from the original Asch experiments show people truly doubting their own vision. And as mentioned in the first lecture of this series, some people are more likely to be concerned about and try to adhere to group norms. Those people are called collectivists.

Collectivists value their connections with the group and will subsume their individual preferences and feelings to the good of the group. Collectivism varies across individuals and across cultures. Certain countries have cultures that promote a higher level of collectivism among their citizens. Countries with high levels of collectivism include Japan and Korea. Countries with low levels of collectivism include the United States, Canada, and Australia. At these extremes, we would observe differences in a way that participants behave in conformity experiments like Asch's. So, the first target characteristic is the cultural characteristic of collectivism. Collectivists will be more likely to be influenced by others within their group in order to preserve harmony and consensus within the group.

The second characteristic of targets that's relative to persuasion is suggestibility. Suggestibility is basically synonymous with gullibility. It's a person's willingness to accept messages from self or others. In effect, it's the likelihood that something that is seen, heard, or felt will immediately be judged as true. There are actually a few different aspects, or dimensions, of suggestibility. One survey measure of it is called the Multidimensional Iowa Suggestibility Scale, MISS or Miss for short, created and owned by professor Roman Kotov as part of his doctoral work at the University of Iowa. It has dimensions that include consumer suggestibility, persuadability, peer conformity, and stubborn opinionatedness. These and other dimensions cover the various ways that information can come to a person and to potentially influence him, from the self, from peers, and from the media.

Let's discuss the four dimensions I just mentioned in turn, along with sample questions that are included in the MISS questionnaire created by Kotov and used in research. First, consumer suggestibility is how easily one is persuaded by messages from the media about products and services. People who score high in this dimension are generally influenced by advertisements and other things they see and hear in the media. Think about yourself as you listen to the following statements, and rate yourself with a number from one to five, where one indicates not at all like me, and five indicates very much like me. Here's the first statement: I often get information about products from commercials. Here's another statement for you to rate: After someone I know tries a new product, I will usually try it too. So, how much do these two statements describe you? If you rated yourself as a four or five, then you are relatively high on consumer suggestibility, and you may find yourself convinced to buy new products more often than other people.

While consumer suggestibility deals with advertisements and commercials, persuadability is how easily one is persuaded by information provided by your peers. People high on this are more easily convinced by others' ideas. Again, let's rate ourselves on a scale from one, not at all like me, to five, very much like me. I can be convinced by a good argument. I get many good ideas from others. It's generally not a bad thing if you can be convinced by a good argument. I wish more people I worked with would be, but if you answered a four or five here, then you are relatively high on persuadability. Now we move to peer conformity. This is how often you conform to your friends and colleagues in order to fit in. People high on this dimension pay attention and generally conform to what people around them are doing. Two more items, rate yourself, again, one being low, and five being high. If you give yourself a four or five, then you're high on peer conformity. My friends and I like the same thing, and, I follow current fashion trends.

A final dimension of suggestibility that I will discuss is stubborn opinionatedness. As reported by professor Kotov, this characteristic has a small but reliable negative correlation with the other dimensions that I mentioned. Having higher levels of this characteristic actually renders you less likely to be influenced by others. Rate yourself on these items: I question what I see on the news. I have strong opinions on most issues. If you gave yourself a high rating of a four or five on these items, then you are generally less suggestible than others. It's easy to witness stubborn opinionatedness in politics and in business. Perhaps the most classic example with the associated positive and negative effects is the late Apple founder and CEO, Steve Jobs. Jobs was known for having strong opinions and to fight with those around him to advance those ideas. It was his greatest strength and his greatest liability. By sticking to his vision of clean, simple, and well-controlled products, he pushed forward the iMac, the iPod, the iPhone, and the iPad, as well as the iTunes store that supports them. Along the way he and his company revolutionized one industry after another, pushing forward the graphical user interface in personal computing, digital music player, and the smartphone. The downside came from many people finding it hard to work for Jobs. When we think about his team trying to influence him as a target, things could get stressful. Jobs would argue and argue and even yell, and many good people left the company because they could not take the stress and the feeling that Jobs' opinion mattered more than theirs. Fortunately, his ideas were good, so he and his company were successful.

Let's review a study that examines how someone high in suggestibility differs from someone who is low on this characteristic. Martin Brüne and his colleagues from Ruhr University Bochum in Germany examined the relationship between suggestibility and acceptance in an ultimatum game. Before research participants played the game, they answered a portion of the suggestibility survey. Then they played. The ultimatum game is used in many decision-making studies and involves two players who interact to decide how they would share money given to them. The typical sequence goes like this. You are told that your partner is being given 10 money units. He offers you some percent of that amount. You can refuse, in which case, no one keeps any of those units, or you can accept, in which case, you both keep the proposed sums.

More concretely, in this study, let me walk you through what would happen if you were a subject. You would be seated at a computer screen and told to watch the screen. The screen would indicate that you and a partner pictured and named on the screen somehow find €10.00 on the street. Your partner picks it up and suggests how the money will be split. On the next screen you can either accept or reject that offer. Again, if you accept, you're told you earn that money. If you reject, neither of you gets any money. At the end of the experiment you are rewarded with an amount that reflects what you decided to keep during the game, so there is a real-world consequence in terms of the money you receive.

As you might imagine, in this ultimatum game, a 50/50 split is considered fair, and everyone agrees. The interesting question is what happens when the proposed split is not fair, say, seven to three—your partner keeps €7.00; you get 3.00—eight to two, or even nine to one. Are you willing to say no even though it means you don't get anything just because you think it's unfair and you don't think the other person should keep any money? In the study by Brüne and colleagues, they found that suggestibility did not matter in the fair split condition. After all, everyone agreed when the split was five and five. Suggestibility also did not really matter in the seven-three split condition either. But in the most unfair situations, when the partner offered an eight-two or a nine-one split, people with higher suggestibility were much more likely than others to say yes to that ultimatum. In other words, those high in suggestibility were willing to acquiesce to what is clearly an unfair proposal. What would you do?

In this study only 16 percent of subjects agreed to the nine-one offer, but the majority of that group was high in suggestibility. So the answer to what you would do probably depends on how you answered the questions that I posed to you earlier. If you were more suggestible, then you were more likely to take an offer, even if it is unfair. Let's think about this finding a bit more broadly. When an opportunity comes up to influence someone and you are the agent, how likely you are to succeed will depend not just on you, but on your target as well. If your target is more suggestible, then you're more likely to win, even if what you're asking isn't really fair. If your target is low on suggestibility, then you may not win even if you are a master at wielding influence. This reinforces the idea that the success of influence is determined by multiple factors, and you cannot guarantee success every single time.

So far, we've looked at two characteristics that make a target more or less susceptible to influence: collectivism and suggestibility. Now let's turn to another important target characteristic: age. Why would age be associated with influence success? The reason is that both younger adults and much older adults are more susceptible to influence. Let's begin with kids. It's commonly believed that children and adolescents are poor critical thinkers and will be more likely to conform with their peers. This is why the answer to your question to your teen child "hey, if Bobby jumped off a cliff, would you?" may not be what you want to hear. Does research support the idea that younger adults are more likely to go along with their friends? Psychologist Laurence Steinberg and Kathryn Monahan, both from Temple University, examined how resistant people were to peer influence. For this survey, participants were given pairs of opposing statements and asked to pick which statement described them better. For example, which of the following two statements is more true of your behavior? Some people go along with their friends just to keep their friends happy, or, other people refuse to go along with what their friends want to do, even though they know it will make their friends unhappy.

The researchers administered this survey with many items like this, along with some other tests, to three different samples of people totaling nearly 4,000 respondents, and they were diverse in all ways, including age. What they found was that preteens and teens were particularly less resistant to peer influence. In other words, they were not able to resist. Being able to resist influence began increasing in the teen years and increased gradually each year until about age 20, where it leveled off. So it appears that there really is something to the idea that the preteen and early teen years are filled with concerns about fitting in with peers, and they're more likely to comply.

Leaving the kids behind, let's turn to older adults. Natalie Denburg and her colleagues at the University of Iowa and the University of Southern California were concerned about the rising number of fraud cases that appear to occur with older adults. We seem to see news stories every day about an older adult being taken advantage of by an unscrupulous sales person, or maybe even by their relatives. Is it really the case that older adults are less able to detect lying and deceit? Denburg's work relies on what has been called the frontal lobe hypothesis of aging. This hypothesis suggests that as people age, changes occur in the prefrontal brain structures that undermine fundamental cognitive functions related to decision making. In some adults these changes are disproportionately high. In the Denburg study, three groups were shown an advertisement for Legacy Luggage that had been reported as deceptive by the Federal Trade Commission. The three groups shown the ad included a group of younger adults, age ranges from 26 to 55; a group of older adults with regular cognitive capacities, these were folks age ranges from 56 to 85; and then a group of older adults, same age, 56 to 85, but those who had been shown to have a common, often-seen reduction in cognitive capacities, and this was judged by a separate task.

Two versions of the Legacy Luggage ad were shown, a full disclosure version and a limited disclosure version. Let me explain those two. In the full disclosure version, the caption under the luggage read,

> "Legacy brings you the finest American quality luggage. After manufacture in Mexico, each piece is carefully inspected in Tennessee at our corporate headquarters before shipping to you."

In the limited disclosure version, the same text was used with the exception of an omission of the phrase "in Mexico." That particular wording was ruled by the FTC to be misleading, as it's likely to convey to consumers that the luggage is a product of U.S. origin. But recall, it was manufactured in Mexico and only inspected in Tennessee. How did the various groups do? With the full disclosure, all three groups picked up that the luggage was not actually manufactured in the U.S. In the limited disclosure condition, though, the older impaired group was significantly more likely to believe the luggage was made in the U.S. And as part of that study the researchers asked about purchase intention. How likely would you be to buy this particular product? And with limited disclosure, the older, impaired group had significantly higher purchase intentions than the other two groups.

So older adults who are experiencing a natural decline in cognitive functioning are less likely to pick up on deceptive advertising and thus more likely to be influenced to make a purchase. This makes older adults who are experiencing cognitive decline a target of choice for unethical agents.

So far we've covered collectivism, suggestibility, and age, both young and old. The last characteristic of influence targets that we'll talk about today is motivation. Motivation is a central element to the study of attitude change, how we go about changing our minds about something. For example, someone might have hated Apple computers, but over time come to love them, or used to think that Latin poetry was boring and then come to admire its austere power. Social psychologists have been studying attitude change for quite some time, and a number of useful theories have emerged. One of those is called dual-process theory. As advanced by Richard Petty and John Cacioppo, this theory suggests that attitudes can change through either a central or peripheral root. Central roots are deliberate and effortful and occur when someone thinks carefully about a topic. The process here is that people collect information, deliberate, and then decide their attitudes towards that topic. Peripheral roots occur outside of attention and awareness. Typically people change their mind via peripheral root when something positive or negative is brought to mind while thinking about the topic. For example, if you aren't paying close attention because I'm telling you all about my latest textbook, then you might say great things about the book if I happen to be feeding you some fantastic snacks at the time. In the absence of attention, the positive experience of snacking while learning about my book may increase your positivity towards it. You in the mood for a little bite to eat?

A now classic study examining central and peripheral processing was published in the *Journal of Consumer Research* in 1983. The study, by Petty, Cacioppo, and their colleague David Schumann, found that people's attitudes after viewing an advertisement could not be predicted solely by argument strength—that's the central route—or by whether a famous endorser was used—that's the peripheral route. You had to consider whether people were motivated to pay attention. When people are made to believe that the information presented was personally relevant because they would be asked about it later, the strength of the argument mattered. Because people were motivated in that condition, they paid attention to the detail of the arguments. In this condition, having a famous endorser did not influence participants' attitudes toward the advertised product.

But when people did not think the material was personally relevant to them because they were unlikely to have anything to do with what they were hearing, the argument quality didn't make a difference. Attitudes were the same whether the arguments were strong or weak, but famous endorsers did make a difference. In other words, when people aren't really paying attention, peripheral cues, like endorsements, make a big difference. When people are paying attention, they pay close enough attention to the argument that its quality matters. Now, if you haven't been paying close attention for the last few minutes, just know this: What I'm saying has been approved by Brad Pitt. Why the endorsement joke? As you've surely seen, product endorsements are commonplace advertising tools. Companies pay good money for them. One endorsement that I found particularly amusing was for the classic perfume Chanel N°5. It pictured none other than a close-up of the handsome actor Brad Pitt. I'm fairly confident that Pitt doesn't wear Chanel, but clearly the executives at Chanel believe that pairing a handsome man with their brand is going to boost sales. And if people are skimming magazines and not paying much attention, it might just work.

In the years since Petty and his colleagues published their paper, there have been new theories and new findings, but the basic idea is sound. People are generally less likely to be influenced by extraneous factors if they're motivated to pay attention to the real argument, the real features of the product, and so on. When targets are not motivated, they're more easily influenced via tactics that have little or nothing to do with the actual argument being used by the influencing agent. Have you ever considered why so many infomercials run on late night TV? My first thought was that was the only time these companies could afford advertising, but TV-sold merchandise is big industry. There are actually entire channels devoted to it now. It turns out that one major reason to run late-night infomercials is that viewers are often tired, and thus more likely to be influenced to buy the next greatest thing because of its exhaustive and hard-to-remember list of amazing features. And the positive energy of the person selling surely helps boost influence through the peripheral root. Do I really need this new device? Who knows? But late at night I'm more likely to be persuaded because I'm too tired to give my full attention.

What we've been saying about age and motivation is further supported by a 2011 review by scholars Guang-Xin Xie and David Boush. Their review found that certain people are more likely to believe false claims in ads. Consistent with dual-process theory, people who are either distracted or not motivated are more likely to be susceptible. The authors also find support for age as an important factor. Memory deficits in older adults increase the likelihood that a deceptive ad will be believed.

In this lecture we've discussed characteristics of targets that make them more susceptible to influence, including deceptive influence that we find in misleading advertisements. Of course, whether a particular influence attempt works will depend on other factors that we discuss in other lectures, such as the characteristics of the agent, the tactic, and the context. But all other things equal, the easiest person to influence is someone who is collectivistic, suggestible, either quite young or quite old, and someone not particularly motivated to pay close attention. This is incredibly important information to have. It can help you better understand if you or one of your loved ones is more likely to be influenced. Having that knowledge can help you thwart an influence attempt when it is against your best interest.

What can you do to be less susceptible to influence, particularly if you discover you're prone to it? Stephen Greenspan, in his book *The Annals of Gullibility*, offers four suggestions. First, he argues, make it a point to avoid acting impulsively. Don't make big decisions without sleeping on it. Second, design your own situations to avoid being pressured. Don't shop in stores with pushy sales people or just shop online instead. Third, accept that you don't know everything. By this, Greenspan, I think, is suggesting that you should be willing to ask lots of questions and do additional research before you believe a particular claim. Don't assume that what you have been given as information is all you need to know. Do additional research. And fourth, Greenspan encourages people to become more socially aware, paying careful attention to some of the characteristics and ploys of influence agents that have bad intentions.

Consistent with Greenspan's suggestions, the first thing I will suggest for you to do as you reflect on this lecture is figure out if you are high on suggestibility. A short 21-item version of the MISS scale is available for free online. Take the test to find out where you rank on the various dimensions of suggestibility. If you're high, then you should be extra vigilant about overbuying or following friends into purchases that you don't really need. You should also be mindful, be willing to walk away from a store before you choose to buy. And definitely don't shop when you're tired or hungry.

The second thing I will suggest is particularly important if you are an older adult who's noticed a difference in your memory and processing speed. This is something we should all practice regardless of age. Here is my advice: When you're about to make your next purchasing decision, step back, take some extra time. If someone pushes you to make a decision quickly, you might ask, "If you're really concerned with my best interests, why are you in such a rush to close the sale?" Before making big purchases or big decisions, get second opinions from people who have less of a vested interest in closing the deal. If you see something advertised and it appeals to you, do some secondary research in places like *Consumer Reports* before buying.

In this lecture, we've discussed targets of influence, and how it's important to consider them as part of any influence effort. In the next lecture we'll get to the second T of the ATTiC model, and that's the really fun bit. We'll be talking about the actual influence tactics that we use to get our way.

Influence Tactics—Hard and Soft
Lecture 5

So far in this course, we've discussed both the positive and negative characteristics of agents that determine their use of influence and their success in influencing others. We've also looked at characteristics that make influence targets more or less susceptible to influence attempts. In this lecture, we will consider the second T in our ATTiC model: tactics. We'll focus on what has been learned about general approaches to winning people over. Most of the research we'll consider has been done in work settings, but these influence tactics can be used in your personal life, as well.

Hard and Soft Influence Tactics
- Organizational scholars have studied a series of tactics that people use to convince others at work. According to a 2011 study by Kevin Mullaney at the University of Illinois, most of these different tactics can be put into two categories: hard and soft.

- Hard tactics threaten the autonomy of the target; they attempt to get someone to think or do something specific by metaphorically pushing them in that direction. These tactics include making reference to formal authority, building a coalition, and applying pressure.

- In contrast, soft tactics support the autonomy of the target; they attempt to get someone to think or act in a certain way by making that alternative more appealing than others. These tactics include attempting to persuade with reason or with emotion, complimenting the target (ingratiation), and offering an exchange.

Outcomes of Influence Tactics
- In the first lecture of this course, we discussed three possible outcomes of an attempt to influence: commitment, compliance, and conflict.

- Professor Gary Yukl from the University at Albany has studied influence tactics extensively over the last 20 years. He developed a survey, the Influence Behavior Questionnaire (IBQ), that asks employees to rate how often their supervisors use nine influence tactics, both hard and soft.

- In one study using the IBQ, Yukl and Professor Bruce Tracey of Cornell University asked managers to distribute surveys to their employees, their peers, and their supervisors. Everyone who received a survey rated the managers on influence attempts and the effectiveness of influence efforts. More than 1,000 people filled out surveys for the 128 managers in the study. Yukl and Tracey found small differences in the kinds of tactics people use depending on whether they are trying to influence a subordinate, peer, or supervisor.
  - o Among other findings, the managers in the study used rational persuasion more often with their bosses than with their subordinates and coalition less often with their subordinates than with anyone else.

  - o These results seem to capture the power dynamics in most work organizations: Managers don't often need to develop strong arguments or coalitions to get employees to do their work.

- Two of the nine tactics in the Yukl and Tracey study consistently and positively related to an outcome of commitment. These were the soft tactics of rational persuasion and inspirational appeal.

Rational Persuasion
- Essentially, rational persuasion is about putting forward ideas for why a particular course of action is a good one and should be the way forward. When a mother tells a child to do something because she said so, she's not using rational persuasion. When you give a coworker three reasons to change a procedure, you're using rationality.

- A 2003 meta-analysis published in the *Journal of Organizational Behavior* found that rationality (as a general tactic) has the strongest positive effect on work outcomes. In short, it is a good first "go to" tactic for getting commitment from people you are trying to influence at work.

- In many cases, doing a little research and preparing a list of reasons before an influence attempt can save time and streamline the process of change over using the hard tactic of pressure.

Inspiration
- Inspiration is about using appeals to value and higher-order principles to motivate action. When you tell a child to do something for the sake of safety, you're using pressure, not inspiration. When you tell a target that working together will help make the world a better place for children, then you're using inspiration.

- In raising money for a daycare center, an appeal to parents could point out the benefits of keeping tuition low while still paying teachers competitive salaries. Such an appeal is rational. But to convince parents to commit both time and money to the daycare center, a more appropriate appeal might be to highlight the remarkable sense of community fostered by the center and its ability to create a challenging and loving environment for children. This is an appeal to emotion and principle, not just reason.

- People follow inspirational leaders, such as Gandhi and Martin Luther King. Both of these men put themselves in a position to stand for a principle; when they asked their followers to take risks, they were asking them to serve a higher goal. Gandhi and Dr. King inspired people to work toward the dream of a better future, which is a powerful motivator for hard work and risk-taking behavior.

Listening: A Key to Successful Influence
- In their book *Real Influence*, Mark Goulston and John Ullmen emphasize the need to avoid hard tactics and offer tips for using soft tactics and gaining commitment. The core of their argument is quite simple: To gain commitment, agents have to listen in order to adjust their influence efforts to account for their targets' thoughts

One of the secrets to using rational persuasion and inspiration effectively is simply listening to your targets.

and feelings. The authors interviewed more than 100 high-level influencers and found that listening and adjusting are keys to success.

- Goulston and Ullmen's book is compelling because it does not give a specific formula for influence. Instead, it recommends learning as much as you can about the people involved in a given situation and understanding their views.

- With this information, you will discover how to frame your message—the persuasive reasons and the inspirational emotion—in a way that is tailored directly to the target and the context at hand.

Using Hard Tactics
- In some circumstances, commitment isn't a feasible or a necessary outcome. If you are primarily concerned with expedient, short-term compliance, then hard tactics may be appropriate. But as all parents know, putting a foot down hard can result in resistance!

- In some settings, hard tactics are necessary—especially when the issue is truly important and time is of the essence. If you want to stop a child from running into the street, you need to act quickly, and you use hard tactics precisely because you are looking out for the best interests of the child. In business, if your company is risking the loss of a great deal of money because of inaction and other tactics have failed, it may be time for some pressure.

- Gary Yukl's most recent work supports the idea that good managers are flexible and adapt their influence tactics to the demands of different situations. On area of day-to-day business in which this advice can be fruitfully applied is discipline. A technique called "discipline without punishment" combines soft and hard tactics in a way that is consistent with Yukl's advice to be flexible.

  o The idea of discipline without punishment was developed by Dick Grote. The goal is to motivate employees to choose better behavior and commit to it, but if they don't do so, to move them out the door.

  o Grote suggests that when a problem occurs with an employee, the manager should meet with the employee to identify the discrepancy between actual and desired performance, explain the reasons the employee's behavior must change, and seek agreement to change. Notice the use of rational persuasion here.

  o If bad performance continues, the manager has a second, more in-depth meeting to provide further explanations and reconfirm the employee's commitment to change. This continues the rational persuasion but begins to apply pressure, because the manager explains that the absence of change is a serious concern.

  o As the last step in this process, if unsatisfactory behavior continues, the employee is given a full paid day off to encourage thought. Giving a paid day off removes hostility from the situation and helps the employee realize that the manager is making an investment in his or her ability to change. Employees are asked to "consider their future with the organization and decide if they are willing to meet standards." This is a combination of exchange (the employee is getting something) and pressure (the employee is told to consider not returning if he or she is not willing or able to change).

o   This process requires the intentional use of a few different tactics, and it follows clear and deliberate steps that encourage the employee to play an active role. When done properly, it places the employee in an empowered position to choose between continued behavior and job loss or changed behavior and job retention.

Application: Building Influence Skills

- The next time you are trying to convince someone else to take action, stop to consider your own reasons for desiring a certain response from the other person—and then disregard those reasons. Think about the reasons that your target should want to take action. Those are the reasons you should use as the basis of your effort to persuade!

- As a second activity, ask a trusted friend or family member for feedback about how often you use hard and soft influence tactics. Do you make use of the more effective tactics—rational persuasion and inspirational appeal—consistently? Ask for advice about improving your tactics. Interestingly, consultation is an influence tactic of its own that has received some recent research attention. Consulting with others to get the information and ideas that will help you improve may actually help you build relationships that will allow for better influence outcomes in the future.

Suggested Reading

Goulston and Ullmen, *Real Influence.*

Grote, *Discipline without Punishment.*

1. The next time you are trying to convince someone else to take action, consider your own reasons for desiring a certain response. Then, discard those reasons. Consider the reasons that your target should want to take action. Use those points as the basis for your effort to persuade.

2. Ask trusted friends or family members how often they see you using hard and soft influence tactics. Do you consistently use the more effective tactics—rational persuasion and inspirational appeal? Ask for advice about how you could be better at persuading.

Real-World Scenario

Suppose you're asked to generate excitement about a new product among an existing team of salespeople. The team is already in place, and you are the outsider bringing in change. Everything you've heard suggests that this will be a tough job; this team has a reputation for sticking together and rejecting outsiders. What can you do to convince the members to get on board?

You should begin with listening and learning. Listening can be more difficult than it appears at first because you will bring many assumptions and biases to the situation. We all have the natural tendency to engage in selective listening to support what we already believe. Thus, in your first few days on the team, you are likely to come to the conclusion that everything you heard was right, and this team hates you.

But if you reach out and try to connect with the salespeople individually, you will learn a great deal about the team. For example, the reputation for rejecting outsiders might stem from having a string of bad supervisors in rapid succession. You might learn that the team members like and respect one another because they have a long history together, and they may worry that an outsider will spoil their camaraderie.

Goulston and Ullmen suggest that to be influential, you have to begin with an understanding of the team members' perspectives. Learn how they perceive the situation, in this case, a new supervisor, a new product, and perhaps, other changes. Continue the effort to understand by asking the team members' opinions about the best way to move forward. Only when you see things from their point of view can you begin to see how you might move them from their way of thinking to an alternative.

In the case of the new product, the salespeople may believe that they already work well together and don't need much at all from a new supervisor to discover how this new product will fit into the existing line. In other words, what this team wants from you is support and protection from outside influence, not meddling in the team's day-to-day business. If this is how the situation plays out, then your job may be easier than you thought, but to figure that, you must be willing to set aside your assumptions and biases and listen to the team members' perspective.

Influence Tactics—Hard and Soft
Lecture 5—Transcript

Let me tell you about a story. Someone I worked with on a nonprofit board, she was bright, personable, always helped move conversations along with an energetic style and a can-do attitude. I remember liking her right away and being glad that I had the opportunity to work with her side by side. When the nonprofit organization that we were working for had a crisis and needed a new building, she used her connections and charm to locate a great possibility for us. In fact, it was the one we ultimately pursued. We bought that building and began remodeling. She worked many evenings and hours to help renovate the facility so we would be ready for the big opening, literally using hammer, saw, and screwdrivers to move things along.

She sounds like the ideal manager, the ideal board member for a small nonprofit like this one. She did have a weakness, though, and it turned out to be a big one. When people disagreed with her and it came time for her to convince them that her ideas were the best, she would get irritated, raise her voice, and essentially demand that things go her way. I remember one time when a volunteer came to discuss how money from a fundraiser she ran should be allocated. My colleague disagreed, and when our volunteer didn't fall in line, my colleague literally got out of her chair and yelled.

So far in this course we've discussed both the positive and negative characteristics of agents that determine their use and success of influence. We've also looked at characteristics that make influence targets more or less susceptible to influence attempts. In the ATTiC model we're using in this course, it's time to consider the second T, tactics. Does the tactic used by my colleague, yelling and demanding her way, actually work? We hear stories of bosses yelling; we see it on TV, and perhaps you've even experienced it yourself. Is pressuring someone with an angry voice the best way to bring people to your way of thinking?

Research has a great deal to say about this, and that research will be the focus for this lecture. In a later lecture we'll talk about the field of rhetoric, which is the use of language to persuade. For now, we'll focus on what has been learned about general approaches to win people over. Most of the research we'll discuss today has been done in work settings, but these influence tactics can be used in your personal life as well. As a preview to the research findings we'll discuss, I can tell you what happened in the case of my colleague and her yelling episode. The person on the receiving end of the yelling did not change her mind, and she was willing to yield to the argument of that day. She left in line with what my yelling colleague would later say is the right way of thinking, but she also left a little scared and a lot frustrated. What happened next is telling. After initially complying, she later vowed to never help our organization again. So while my colleague may have made her point, it was a Pyrrhic victory. She won the battle that day, but in the process, lost an important volunteer and supporter of our organization.

Organizational scholars have studied a series of tactics that people use to convince others at work. According to a 2011 study by Kevin Mullaney at the University of Illinois, most of these different tactics can be put into two categories, hard and soft. Hard tactics threaten the autonomy of the target. They attempt to get someone to think or do something specific by metaphorically pushing them in that direction. These tactics include making reference to formal authority, I'm your boss and my role is to set your job responsibilities; building a coalition, I've talked to all the colleagues here and we all agree; or applying pressure, you have to do this or else. You can see these play out in parent-child relationships too with phrases like, do it because I told you, and I'm your father; or, your mom and I agree this is what you must do; or finally, if you don't get moving right now, I'm taking away your cell phone for a week.

Let me tell you a story of a hard tactic used in a work setting. Imagine Bob as a team leader trying to motivate his team to work hard to meet a project deadline. He wants to influence them to stay late and work all night to get details right. Here is one effort using a hard tactic. Team, this is it. We've got to get this project done by tomorrow. I'll be here all night, and if I'm here, you will be too. I won't hear another word about it. Let's get to work. That's the hard tactic of pressure. I've seen it used quite a few times. My colleague's yelling seems to fit that category, doesn't it?

Let's contrast that with a soft tactic. Soft tactics support the autonomy of the target. They attempt to get someone to think or act in a certain way by making that alternative more appealing than others. These tactics include attempting to persuade with reason or emotion, saying nice things about the person, what we call ingratiation, or offering something in exchange. Let's listen to what a soft tactic would sound like. Imagine a different team leader, Pat, in the same situation I used before. Team, this is it. We've got to get this project done by tomorrow. Now, I know how tough overtime can be on you and your family; we all have important commitments outside this room, but if we all work together we can win this one. Let's do it and make each other proud. Pat's effort to persuade relies on inspiration. Just listening to her you feel a whole lot better about the idea of working late.

A few studies help identify outcomes of hard and soft tactics. But let's review again some material we discussed in the very first lecture of this course. What are the possible outcomes of an influence attempt? Remember there were three, all beginning with C. First, commitment, and that's usually the desired goal. Commitment is when someone agrees with you and becomes convinced that what you're proposing is the right way to go. Your target commits to think or act the way you intend. The second C is compliance. This is usually acceptable, but less than ideal. Compliance is when someone agrees for the sake of agreeing, and they'll do what's being asked, but certainly not with enthusiasm. The problem here is that you really haven't convinced the target. And once the winds blow in a different way, you may not get what you want any longer. Can you recall the third, which is really a failure of influence? It's conflict. That's generally the opposite of what you hope to achieve; rather than getting the desired thought or behavior, you get a fight.

So what tactics do people generally use at work, and which tactics do they generally prefer to see used on them at work? And what tactics generally lead to commitment, compliance, and conflict? Professor Gary Yukl from the University of Albany has studied influence tactics extensively over the last 20 years. He developed a questionnaire called the Influence Behavior Questionnaire, IBQ for short. The survey is given to employees who are asked to rate how often their supervisor uses one of nine influence tactics. Yukl's IBQ asks about both hard and soft tactics that we discussed earlier. In one particular study using the IBQ, Yukl and Professor Bruce Tracey of Cornell University, asked managers to distribute surveys to their employees, their peers, and their supervisor. Everyone who received a survey rated the managers on influence attempts and the effectiveness of those efforts. Over 1,000 people filled out surveys for the 128 managers who were participating. What did the results indicate?

First, Yukl and Tracey found that small differences existed in the kinds of tactics people used, depending on whether they were trying to influence a subordinate, a peer, or a supervisor. Among other things, the managers in the study used rational persuasion more often with their bosses than with their subordinates and the coalition tactic less often with their subordinates than with anyone else. These results capture the power dynamics in most work organizations. Managers don't often need to develop strong arguments or coalitions to get their employees to do the work they're supposed to do. That doesn't mean that managers shouldn't. It just means that they tend to use rational persuasion less often with their subordinates than they do with peers or bosses.

The second finding from the Yukl and Tracey study is that, of all these nine tactics, two came out consistently and positively related to the outcome of commitment. These were soft tactics of rational persuasion and inspirational appeal. Let's talk in more detail about each and bring in some additional research to help you become more effective at using them. First, let's talk about rational persuasion. Ultimately, rational persuasion is about putting forward ideas for why a particular course of action is a good one and should be the way that people behave in the future. When you tell someone to do something because you said so, you're not using rational persuasion. When you give someone three reasons why they should do something, that's when you're putting this tactic to good use.

There's additional research indicating the usefulness of this particular tactic. A 2003 meta-analysis published in the *Journal of Organizational Behavior* found that rationality, as a general tactic, has the strongest positive effect on a variety of work outcomes. In short, it is a good first go-to tactic for getting commitment from people you're trying to influence at work. In my own life, I've seen this happen, and I've seen it work, both at work and at home. When trying to convince my colleagues about a curriculum change, which I've done a couple times now, I've had mixed success. In one effort I was hurried, and I remember distinctly just wanting to get done, so I resorted to a hard tactic. I used pressure. These weren't my exact words, but the gist of what I said in a meeting was, Look, people. I didn't even want to do this. Can't you just approve it so we can get done? Let's just say that didn't go over well, and we ended up discussing and discussing the ideas involved in this particular curriculum change for what seemed like forever.

The next time I was involved in a change like that I prepared. I prepared more beforehand by thinking of a list of reasons I thought the change was appropriate for our department, my colleagues, and for our students. As I presented to my peers, I noted these points. I gave the list of reasons. I also listened carefully to their concerns, acknowledging them and analyzing how they fit into what I already learned. That discussion was shorter than my previous attempt, and boy, did it go better. The curriculum was approved.

In the end both of these curriculum changes were approved, so they both worked, but the more successful of the two was definitely when I sought to use a soft tactic of rational persuasion, rather than the hard tactic of pressure. And it actually, in the end, took less time to use rational persuasion. Why? Well, with a little bit of investment up front, with a little bit of work, the conversation that we had was more productive. So when I shifted from hard tactic to soft, the process was smoother.

Now let's look at that second influence tactic that seems to have a strong correlation with commitment—inspiration. Ultimately, inspiration is about using appeals to values, higher order principles to motivate someone to action. When you tell someone to do something to save their skin or get a pay raise, that's more about pressure or exchange. When you tell someone that together you can help make the world a better place, then you're getting inspirational. I've tried to use inspiration in my own attempts at influence. For example, a few years ago I was raising money for my kid's daycare, a local nonprofit. In an appeal to current and former parents of kids at the center, I could have talked about how it's important to raise money to keep tuition down and, boy, our teachers work hard, and they need better pay. That was rational. It would have been an attempt at rational persuasion, and it may have worked. Instead, I opted to try to be inspirational in the hopes of getting the parents to commit time to help fundraise, as well as to open their checkbooks.

I talked about how remarkable of a community the daycare was in its ability to create a challenging and loving environment for my kids. I also told a little story about how much my kids loved this place, specifically about a day when I was given a lecture by my kids. I'd left work a little early. I got there excited to see my kids, and I got the lecture. Dad, you came too early. I wanted to stay and have more fun with my friends. So when raising money, I went on to explain how I had to; I felt obligated and excited to give back something to sustain a community that meant so much to my kids and my family. This type of appeal engages people's emotions and speaks directly to principles of fairness, for example. It's an appeal to emotion and principle, not just to reason.

People follow inspirational leaders. Think about it. What about Gandhi encouraged people to follow him, walking against the police with batons in India? And what was it about Martin Luther King that made people follow him and walk against water hoses in the streets of Birmingham, Alabama? In both these cases, the leaders put themselves in a position to stand for a principle. They stood up for justice and for freedom. So when they asked their followers to take risks, they asked them to serve a higher goal. They inspired people to work toward the dream of a better future, to be part of something bigger than yourself, to work toward a better future. These are powerful motivators. They help people take on risks. They encourage people to work hard, and they help accomplish great things. We'll revisit inspiration when we talk about leadership in the last lecture of this course.

Now that we've talked about rational persuasion and inspiration, I'd like to discuss one of the secrets to using both tactics successfully. In their book *Real Influence*, Mark Goulston and John Ullmen really emphasize the need to avoid hard tactics. They offer tips for using soft tactics and gaining commitment. The core of their argument is really quite simple, and that is, to gain commitment, you have to listen. You have to listen so you can learn and adjust your influence efforts to what your target is thinking and feeling. The authors interviewed over 100 high-level influencers, as they call them, and found that listening and adjusting are key. Let me walk you through an example. Suppose you're asked to lead an existing team of sales people, to get them excited about a new product that they'll have to sell. The team is already in place, and you're the outsider bringing in the change, the new product. Everything you've heard in advance suggests that this is going to be a tough job. This team has a reputation for loving each other and hating outsiders like you. What can you do to convince them to come together, get on board, and really push forward this project?

Well, you should begin with listening and learning. Listening could actually be tougher than it first appears because you'll bring many assumptions and biases to this situation. We all have a natural tendency to engage in selective listening to support what we already believe. So in your first few days on the team, you're likely to simply come to the conclusion that everything you heard was right, and this team hates you. But if you reach out and connect with members of the team individually, really trying to understand who they are, what they're concerned about, what they're thinking, then you will learn a great deal about the team. You might learn that hating outsiders as a reputation really comes from a history that they have of a string of three nasty supervisors that span through over the years of their group. You might learn that team members really like and respect each other because they have a long history together. In short, they trust each other, and they worry that an outsider, someone like you, will ruin it.

Goulston and Ullmen suggest that to be influential you'll have to understand your team members' perspectives and begin there. So that means beginning with an understanding of how they see the situation. In this case, how do they see you, their new supervisor? How do they see the product and the other changes going on with the company? And the effort to understand must continue with you taking their perspective about the best way forward. Only when you see things from their point of view can you begin to see how you might move them from their way of thinking to an alternative way of thinking. In the case of a team or a new product, they may see a way forward already. They already work well together—they don't need much at all from you as a supervisor. In other words, what this team wants from you is support and protection from outside influence, not meddling in their day-to-day business. If this is how the situation plays out, then your job may be a whole lot easier than you thought. It's about support, rather than about trying to teach them or push them to do something new.

I find Goulston and Ullmen's book quite compelling, because it doesn't really offer a simple formula for influence. It does not tell you that you should use rational persuasion here or inspiration here. It tells you that you have to learn as much as you can about the people involved and understand how they see the world and the situation. With this information you'll be able to understand how to set up messages, how to be persuasive, how to be inspirational in ways that are tailored directly to the target and context at hand.

Okay. So we've discussed two of the most effective tactics at gaining commitment. On average, rational persuasion and inspirational appeal are your best options. But we've talked about how listening and perspective taking are magic ingredients that help make those soft tactics work. Where does this leave hard tactics? Should you avoid them altogether? There are circumstances when commitment simply isn't a feasible or necessary outcome. If you are primarily concerned with expedient short-term compliance, then hard tactics may be appropriate. But as all parents know, putting a foot down hard can result in resistance. If you're dealing with friends or employees, the power dynamic is a bit different than with kids. Kids can't choose their parents, but at work, boy, your best employees? They often can find their way to the door.

So when are hard tactics and the resulting compliance reasonable approaches? In some settings hard tactics are necessary, especially when the issue is important or time is of the essence. If you want to get a child out of the street or make sure that she rides with a helmet on. Time is of the essence, and you use hard tactics precisely because you're looking out for the best interests of the child. There are equivalents in other areas of life. For example, if your company is going to lose a great deal of money because of inaction and other tactics have failed, then it may be time for some pressure. If the nonprofit where you volunteer is starting to fail its clients because someone is not doing his job correctly, then it may be time to use hard tactics, like pressure or appeals to authority.

Because hard tactics may be called for, rarely, but certainly at times, it's worth considering that good managers and leaders are ultimately flexible in how they use influence. Gary Yukl's most recent work supports the idea that great managers are flexible. They adapt their influence tactics to the demands of different situations that they face. Let me quote Yukl directly. Good leaders "diagnose the situation and identify the types of behaviors that are appropriate. They know how to use many different behaviors skillfully." To follow Yukl's suggestions here, it's necessary to go into a situation where influence is called for with an open mind. You have to be willing to change things up in how you use influence tactics. One area of day-to-day business life where this can certainly, fruitfully, be applied is in the area of employee discipline. The worst part of a manager's job is telling someone that he is doing the wrong things, or doing things wrong. There's some guidance in this particular task that combines soft and hard tactics in a way that is consistent with Yukl's advice to be flexible.

The technique is called discipline without punishment and the person who developed it, Dick Grote, not only wrote a book about the technique, he also implemented it in his own job. The goal of discipline without punishment is to get employees to choose better behavior and commit to it, but if they don't do so, to move that person out the door. Here's what Grote suggests. When an employee problem occurs, the manager begins with a face-to-face meeting. The manager meets with the employee in order to figure out what the discrepancy is between actual and desired performance, explain the reasons behavior needs to change, and seek agreements that the change will happen. Notice here the use of rational persuasion.

If bad performance continues, the manager has a second, more in-depth meeting to provide further explanations and to reconfirm the employee's commitment to change. This continues the rational persuasion, but begins to apply some pressure, as it should be explained that the absence of change, the failure to do something different, will result in some action. As the last step in this process, much akin to a three-strikes policy, if unsatisfactory behavior continues, the employee is given a full paid day off. A day off? The goal of the paid day off is to remove hostility and help the employee sit and think, to see the manager is investing in them. Employees are asked a very specific question: Consider your future with this organization and decide if you are willing to meet our standards.

This is a combination of exchange, the employee is actually getting something, and pressure. The employee is told that they should consider not coming back if they're not willing or able to change. This process requires the intentional use of a few different tactics. It follows clear and deliberate steps that encourage employees to play an active role, making choices about how they're going to be at work. When done properly, it places the employee in an empowered position. Grote's book reviews positive outcomes that he and others have had using discipline without punishment in a number of companies. The ideas really are very consistent and quite useful, even working with children.

In this lecture I've presented information on hard and soft tactics and provided some guidance on why soft tactics are generally preferable. I also argued that you can make soft tactics work best by listening and taking the other person's perspective. And we found that, ultimately, we should be flexible and willing to use a variety of tactics, such as in the case of discipline without punishment.

As always, I will conclude the lecture with two things that you can try in order to build your skills as an ethical persuader. First, next time you find yourself wanting someone else to do something, stop to consider the reasons why you want them to do it; list them, and then throw those reasons out the window. Now, think about the reasons why they should want to do that. Those are the reasons that you should use as a basis for your efforts to persuade using rational persuasion, inspiration, or both.

The second thing you can try is to ask a trusted friend or family member for feedback. How often do they see you using hard and soft influence tactics? Do you make use of more effective tactics, rational persuasion and inspirational appeal, regularly? Ask for their advice about how you could be better at persuading. This is actually an influence tactic in and of itself. It's called consultation. Consulting with others to get information that will help you get better will help you build a better relationship with that person and also allow you to have better influence outcomes in the future.

In this lecture you've learned a bit about different influence tactics. In the next lecture, we'll build on the foundation we've laid today by talking about specific suggestions for making soft tactics as effective as possible. We'll answer the question, what additional things need to be in place for my chosen influence tactic to succeed.

How to Make the Most of Soft Tactics
Lecture 6

In our last lecture, we concluded that soft influence tactics generally work better than hard influence tactics. That is, you can be more effective in influencing others by making your suggested course of action more appealing, rather than by pressuring your targets. We also saw that soft tactics generally rely on providing rational arguments or emotionally laden information to get others to see that your way of doing things makes sense. In this lecture, we'll delve deeper into the use of soft tactics and learn what we can do to make them work even better. As we'll see, two important characteristics of agents that affect how well tactics work are the agent's power base and political skill.

Power Bases

- Power is generally defined as the capacity for acting or doing. In this regard, power and influence are related but not quite the same. Power is something that an agent possesses, and influence tactics are what an agent chooses to do to apply or leverage power to change someone else's mind or behavior.

- In a classic research article published in 1959, John French and Bertram Raven highlighted five forms of power, later expanding the list to six.
  - Coercive power is based on one's ability to threaten punishment. If you have authority to fire an employee or dock his or her pay, then you have coercive power.

  - Reward power is based on one's ability to promise monetary or nonmonetary compensation. If you have authority to pay a bonus or give time away from work when someone does what you ask, then you have reward power.

  - Legitimate power is based on the presence of formal or informal contracts. In the workplace, legitimate power arises from job descriptions that specify who reports to whom. Usually, this form of power corresponds with coercive and reward power but not always. In some work environments, team leaders manage and coordinate work assignments without being given complete power to punish and reward.

o   Information power is based on one's ability to provide relevant facts and figures. When you have all the relevant facts and know who to talk to, then you have the capacity to provide or withhold information in relation to others who need it. Such information can be acquired in many ways, such as by knowing the right people and actively seeking to learn from them or simply from being in the right place at the right time.

o   Expert power is based on being recognized as having an extensive and relevant knowledge base. This type of power typically occurs as a result of formal education or experience and is not exactly the same as information power. However, expert power can also come from experience. French and Raven, in their article, use the example of a visitor deferring to the expertise of a local when asking for directions.

o   Referent power is based on people identifying with and admiring the agent in question. This power arises from loyalty and affection, and we see it in operation when employees are motivated to help a leader they admire. An example of someone who holds referent power is Sir Richard Branson, the founder and charismatic leader of Virgin Group.

•   It's easy to see connections between these power bases and hard and soft influence tactics. Coercive and reward power provide the base from which someone could use exchange tactics. For example, a supervisor could say, "I will consider the results of this assignment when I calculate bonuses later this year." Legitimate power provides a base from which someone could use pressure. Again, the supervisor might ask, "Do I have to remind you who does the firing around here?"

- Given such obvious connections, why do we distinguish between power and influence?
  - o Many managers today have power given to them by the nature of their positions—coercive, reward, and legitimate power. But when trying to get employees to work harder or work differently, great managers may never draw on those powers. Instead, they may opt for the soft tactic of explaining why a change is needed.

  - o Similarly, a manager may have both expert and referent power but may decide to use reward power via an exchange tactic to get employees to change their behavior. In other words, power and influence rely on each other but are not synonymous.

Positional Power and Influence in Action
- Imagine a situation in which you, a manager, have discovered that your company may lose a client to a competitor. The client is Jim's, and you think he should be worried and act quickly.

- You might say to Jim: "I just found out that your client, Hensley Enterprises, is unhappy and actively shopping around. This is serious, Jim. If you lose Hensley, then you'll be looking for work." As Jim's formal supervisor, you have coercive, reward, and legitimate power bases. In this case, you're leveraging the coercive power base of your position and applying a pressure tactic. You're trying to push Jim into action with a threat.

- There are other ways that you might push Jim into action using power derived from your position. For example, you might try a simple reference to your legitimate power: "Jim, I'm clearing everything else off your plate for the next 48 hours; I want you to get to work on keeping Hensley." Implicit here is the idea that you are the supervisor and you have power over Jim's responsibilities and assignments. This is also a pressure tactic, but it is gentler than the threat of firing.

- As a supervisor, you could also leverage reward power: "Jim, if you keep Hensley on our books, I'll make sure the effort is worth your while at bonus time."

- All of these situations have something in common. The power bases they depict—coercive, reward, and legitimate—derive from the agent's job title and responsibilities. As a result, this group of power bases is referred to collectively as positional power.

Personal Power and Influence in Action
- In the same scenario, with you as the supervisor, you might rely on informational power in dealing with Jim.
  - For example, you could say, "Jim, I just found out that your client, Hensley Enterprises, is unhappy and actively shopping around, including having lunch with a sales superstar from our main competitor. I've also heard that Hensley wants to cut both costs and inventory and is not satisfied with our bulk pricing deal. When is the last time you talked to your contacts at Hensley?"

  - The power base here has nothing to do with your position and everything to do with the information that you've accumulated and are passing along. This situation shows the use of informational power without any particular tactic being applied.

- The expert and referent power bases refer to how the agent is perceived by the target. If Jim sees you, his supervisor, as an expert and you raise questions about the handling of the account, Jim may ask questions to try to learn from you. In the same vein, if Jim admires you and strives to make you proud, then moving Jim to action will be quite easy.

- Expert and referent power, like informational power, are quintessentially personal. As a supervisor, you can use these personal bases of power to influence your employees, rather than relying on your formal position and its associated rewards and punishments.

When working with community committees or neighborhood volunteers, you need to build and leverage personal power to guide people to action.

- Developing personal power bases is not difficult. You can develop expert and informational power by actively seeking information from people and other sources. To gain expert power, seek out experiences, such as extra training or difficult work assignments, that will help demonstrate your knowledge to others.

Political Skill
- Political skill is defined as the ability to understand others and use that understanding to influence others more effectively. Basically, it's the degree to which someone can use influence tactics effectively. Gerry Ferris of Florida State University and his colleagues from around the country identified four dimensions of political skill:
  - Social astuteness: Socially astute individuals comprehend subtle factors in social interactions; they are socially aware and sensitive to the interests of others.

- Interpersonal influence: Individuals who wield interpersonal influence are subtle and convincing in their style, and they do this by being adaptive in their use of tactics.

- Networking ability: Individuals with this skill know how to build and rely on a diverse and extensive network of people. They have many relationships that help them collect information and get things done.

- Apparent sincerity: This dimension of political skill involves the credibility of an individual—the degree to which he or she appears to others to be genuine and to have integrity.

- Research by Ferris and colleagues suggests that social astuteness is particularly important as an overall skill. People who are high on this dimension are rated by supervisors as having better job performance, probably because they are able to work effectively with others and they are good at making sure their bosses see them performing well.

- Apparent sincerity refers to the idea that some people seem genuine and believable; such people are likely to have success with almost any influence effort. In her book *The Personal Credibility Factor*, Sandy Allgeier suggests these steps for gaining credibility:
  - Take the time to learn what you need to know. The connection to informational power is clear here, but this is also about knowing how to do your job well. You cannot overlook the basic issue of being capable of doing what is expected of you.

  - Keep all commitments.

  - Honor confidences and avoid gossip.

  - Know yourself—the good and the bad; show humility and recognize that you have both strengths and weaknesses.

○ Choose to value something in others; show concern and empathy for other people, finding something to appreciate and like. This is a key to building good relationships.

○ Ask questions and listen to the answers. This is the best way to learn.

Application: Developing Power and Credibility

- Referent power is about a relationship you have with others based on respect and admiration. How can you get people to respect you? As a start, initiate conversations with people you hope to influence in the future. Get to know their interests, values, and personal histories. Simply by listening, you will establish relationships based on respect.

- Choose a particular relationship you have (e.g., with a spouse/ significant other, a child, a coworker, or your boss). Now ask yourself: What specific steps can I take to improve my credibility with that person? The key word here is "specific." Don't just regurgitate Allgeier's list. Consider that one way to keep all your commitments is to make fewer and be more realistic about them. Writing down commitments as you make them may be a way to help you keep them.

Suggested Reading

Allgeier, *The Personal Credibility Factor*.

Ferris, et al., "Development and Validation of a Political Skill Inventory."

Pfeffer, *Power*.

Activities to Try

1. Build your referent power. Initiate conversations with people you hope to influence in the future. Make it a point to get to know them as well you can—their interests, values, and personal histories. Simply by listening, you will establish a relationship based on mutual respect.

2. Consider a particular relationship you have (e.g., with a spouse/ significant other, a child, a coworker, or your boss). Now ask yourself: What specific steps can I take to improve my credibility with that person? It's important to be as specific as possible and practice doing one thing better for three weeks.

How to Make the Most of Soft Tactics
Lecture 6—Transcript

In our last lecture we concluded that soft influence tactics generally work better than hard influence tactics. That is, it's better to influence other people by making what you would like them to do more appealing rather than pressuring them. Of course, this is not surprising if you think about your most and least favorite colleague at work. When your least favorite colleague tries to persuade you about something, it's likely that he gets louder and pressures you into seeing things his way. When your most favorite colleague tries to persuade, I'm guessing, she explains, she listens, and then she explains some more. Soft tactics generally rely on providing rational arguments or emotionally laden information to get someone to see that your way of doing or seeing things makes sense.

The focus of this lecture is to delve deeper into the use of soft tactics and ask this question: What can we do to make them work even better? As you probably experienced, soft tactics don't always work. As the father of two preteen girls, I find myself stuck sometimes after 30, 40 minutes of failed rational and emotional appeal. And yes, I occasionally utter those words that I never thought would cross my lips: Because I said so! Which is the quintessential hard tactic, isn't it? Now, I don't do that often, but I think it's useful to admit it. The same thing happens in politics when arguments sometimes fall short and then nothing happens and at work when an appeal to emotion does little to engage people in a new important initiative or project.

The failure of soft tactics occurs for any number of reasons related to the ATTiC model we've been using since the opening lecture. It can be that the tactic is not used effectively, as I suggested in the last lecture when I mentioned the importance of listening and learning about the target. Failure also can be a result of the target. In my case at home, young ladies who, as influence targets, possess what we called stubborn opinionatedness. They simply are hard to convince sometimes. Failure can also occur as a result of other combinations of agent characteristics. It turns out that there are two important characteristics of agents that work in concert with tactics. These are the agent's power base and the agent's political skill. In the remainder of this lecture we'll explore both of these issues, defining the concepts, discussing the research, and offering things you can try so that the next time you seek the high ground with a soft influence tactic, you're even more likely to succeed.

Let's begin by talking about power bases. Power is an important concept, and it's central to many fields of study, including political science, sociology, anthropology, and psychology. It's also a fascinating subject of many art forms. In theatre, for example, many famous plays deal with the motivations behind and the consequences of certain individuals' desire for power. Shakespeare's Macbeth, for example, is considered one of his darkest tragedies. It follows the Scottish Lord Macbeth as he struggles with choices about how to fulfill his own, and his wife's, ambitions for power. In the end, he chooses murder, and if you've seen the play, murder, after murder, after murder. The play is perhaps best considered a study in the most dramatic use of hard influence tactics.

Power is generally defined as the capacity for acting or doing. In this regard, power and influence are related, but not quite the same thing. Power is something that an agent possesses, and influence tactics are what an agent chooses to do to apply or leverage power to get something done. In a classic research article published in 1959, John French and Bertram Raven made clear that there really is not just one form of power, but actually five. They later expanded this list to six forms, or what they call bases of power. We'll briefly review the six main power bases and then discuss how they relate to the effective use of influence tactics. So what are the six forms of power that French and Raven identified?

(1) Coercive power, this power is based on one's ability to threaten punishment. If you have authority as someone's manager to fire that person or dock their pay, then you have coercive power.

(2) Reward power, this power is based on one's ability to promise monetary or nonmonetary compensation. If you have authority to pay a bonus or give time away from work when someone does what you ask, then you have reward power.

(3) Legitimate power, this power is based on the presence of formal or informal contracts. In the workplace, this arises from job descriptions that specify who reports to whom and who has authority over whom. If someone is your direct responsibility at work and you have authority to alter that person's work assignments, then you have legitimate power. Usually this also corresponds with reward and coercive power, but not always. In some work environments there are team leaders who manage and coordinate work assignments without being given complete power to punish and reward.

(4) Information power, this power is based on one's ability to provide relevant facts and figures. I'm sure you've heard the phrase, "information is power," and in today's information economy, it can certainly be true. When you have all the relevant facts and you know who to talk to, then you have the capacity to provide or withhold that information to others who need it to get their job done. Such information can be acquired in lots of different ways, such as by getting to know the right people, actively seeking to learn from them, or simply by being in the right place at the right time.

(5) Expert power, this power is based on being recognized as having an extensive and relevant knowledge base. This type of power typically occurs as a result of formal education or experience and is not exactly the same as information power, which can arise in many other ways, as I mentioned a minute ago. But expert power can also come from experience. French and Raven, in their seminal article, used the example of a visitor deferring to the expertise of a local when asking for directions; that's expert power.

(6) Referent power, this power is based on people identifying with and admiring the agent in question. This is power that arises from loyalty and affection, and you see it in operation when employees want to be around and help someone they admire. An example is Sir Richard Branson, the founder and charismatic leader of Virgin Group, which is a holding company for over 400 companies. Branson started his first company when he was just 15 years old. He's described again and again by those who know and work for him as being loved and admired. In one of his books, *Screw it, Let's do it*, Branson suggests that the secrets to his success in business are a desire to have fun and a willingness to let people around him try just about anything. He wrote

that his Virgin staff called him Dr. Yes; that was his nickname. Now that's a man with referent power.

It's easy to see connections between these power bases and the hard and soft influence tactics we discussed in the last lecture. Coercive and reward power provide the base from which someone could use exchange tactics: Consider what happens next when I decide bonuses later this year; that's what you might say. Legitimate power provides a base from which someone could use pressure: Do I have to remind you who does the hiring and firing around here? Given such obvious connections, why do we distinguish between power and influence? The reason is simple. Many managers today have power given to them by nature of their position—coercive power, reward power and legitimate power—but when trying to get employees to work harder or differently great managers may never draw on those powers. Instead, they may opt for a soft tactic of sitting down and explaining why a change is needed. That's rational persuasion, right? Similarly, a manager who may have both expert and referent power, but for some reason decides to use reward power via some exchange tactic, that's an option as well. In other words, power and influence rely on each other, but they are not synonymous.

Let me illustrate this by using a concrete example. Let's imagine a manager who could use a whole host of power bases with his employees; we'll call him Jim. I'll play the role of the manager to show how different power bases play out with different tactics. The situation is that I, as the manager, have discovered that the company may lose a client to a competitor. The client is Jim's, and I think he should be worried and act quickly, so here's what I say to him: I just found out that your client, Hensley Enterprises, is unhappy and actively shopping around. Damn it, Jim. If you lose Hensley, then you'll be looking for work. As Jim's formal supervisor, I have coercive, reward, and legitimate power bases. In this case, I leveraged the coercive power base in my position and applied a pressure tactic. I'm trying to push Jim into action with a threat.

There are other ways that I might push Jim into action using power derived from my position. I might try a simple reference to my legitimate power: Jim, I just found out that your client, Hensley Enterprises, is unhappy and actively shopping around. I'm clearing everything else off your plate for the next 48 hours. Get to work keeping the Hensley account. Implicit in this statement is that I am the supervisor and I have power over your responsibilities and assignments. And there's also a little bit of a pressure tactic here, but it's certainly gentler than the threat of firing. I could also leverage my reward power here: Jim, I just found out that your client, Hensley Enterprises, is unhappy and actively shopping around. If you keep them on our books I'll make sure it's worth your while at bonus time.

How effective do you think each of these three particular combinations of power bases and tactics would be? Having taught this material for years and having seen many young managers trying to connect power and influence tactics and do it well, I would say that each of these would move Jim into action. In short, I would get compliance because I'm Jim's supervisor. The firing threat, because it is so blatantly a pressure tactic that undermines the relationship between Jim and his boss, is more likely to generate resistance and create problems in the long run, but it may certainly work in the short run.

All of these situations have something in common. The power bases they depict—coercive, reward, and legitimate—all derive from the agent's job title and responsibilities. As a result, we refer to this group of power bases collectively as positional power. When you're selecting influence tactic, it's important to consider whether you have the appropriate power base to use a particular tactic. Consider for a minute what would happen if one of Jim's buddies, also a sales agent, was worried about the department's bonus and wanted Jim to move quickly to save the account. Picture him, again, one of Jim's buddies, coming up to him and saying, "I just found out Hensley Enterprises is unhappy and actively shopping around. If you lose Hensley, then you'll be looking for work." This pressure tactic coming from a coworker rather than a boss would come across as odd. I can imagine Jim saying, what are you talking about? First, how do you know about Hensley? And second, are you threatening me? The awkwardness of this encounter shows how important it is to consider one's power base before selecting an influence tactic. A mismatch between the two is, at worst, likely to create resistance. At best, you just won't be successful, and you'll give the people around you a laugh for the day.

We've discussed the first three of the six power bases. Let's see how the next three—informational, expert, and referent—are different. Let me go back to our scenario and show you what I might say when relying on informational power. Jim, I just found out that your client, Hensley Enterprises, is unhappy and actively shopping around, including having lunch with a sales superstar from our main competitor. Losing that account would be tough on you, your team, and our company. They are our second largest client, and without them, we'd be lucky to hit any of our targets this quarter. Here's what I heard through our mutual friend. The bulk pricing deal we're using isn't cutting costs enough for them, and it pushes them to keep more inventory than they want in stock. I hear that they want to cut costs and inventory so they can downsize their warehouse and get their costs under control. When's the last time you talked with them?

That was a lot of information, and that's the power base of information. It has nothing to do with the position and everything to do with information that's been accumulated as being passed along. That shows how informational power can be used without necessarily applying a particular influence tactic. The end result is likely that Jim will be spurred into action without me having to say anything more. And best of all, with regard to influence, any solution that Jim now comes up with will be one that he has commitment to follow through on, because he will have come up with it all on his own.

I'm not going to read quotes for the last two power bases—expert and referent—because it's hard to depict those power bases in action. Those power bases refer to how the agent is perceived by the target. If Jim sees his supervisor as an expert, and his supervisor raises questions about the handling of the Hensley account, Jim will likely ask lots of questions trying to learn from his supervisor. In the same vein, if Jim really admires his supervisor and constantly strives to make him proud, then moving Jim to action should be quite easy for the supervisor.

Expert and referent power, like informational power, are quintessentially personal. Jim's supervisor can use these personal bases of power to influence him, rather than relying on his formal position and its associated rewards and punishments. Obviously, when dealing outside of formal work arrangements, such as when you volunteer or you're working with your family, you have to rely on personal and not positional power. When working with community committees or with neighborhood volunteers, you don't really have rewards and punishments that you can dole out. You need to build and leverage personal sources or bases of power to bring people together and guide them to action.

Even within formal work environments, though, personal power bases are really useful. There are many, many encounters in the work place where you can't, and probably shouldn't, rely on position power, such as when you deal with your peers or with your boss. In these cases, having paid attention to and developed your personal power bases—gaining information, learning to become an expert, building relationships based on mutual respect—will provide power bases that help you in all situations. And developing these power bases does not involve some mystical practice. You can develop expert and informational power bases by actively seeking information from people and other sources. Make it a point to read the newspaper, ask questions of those around you, and seek to meet new people at work. For expert power you have to consider not just what you know, but whether it is perceived as granting you status as "expert." Consider the people whom you want to influence. What would they consider to mark or distinguish experts? Would a particular degree or an online certificate make a difference? Or would a particular work assignment do the trick? Seek out the experiences and education that will demonstrate to others that you possess expert power.

Now that we've covered the topic of power, it's time to move to our second major agent characteristic that interacts with tactics to determine success or failure—political skill. The political skill of an agent is just as important as power bases, and like personal power, it is something that can be developed over time. Political skill is defined as the ability to effectively understand others and use that understanding to better influence them. Given this definition, it's easy to see why this is such an important idea to discuss. Political skill is basically the degree to which you can effectively use influence tactics.

So what constitutes political skill? Drawing on a series of studies by Gerry Ferris of Florida State University and his colleagues around the country, there are four dimensions. Social astuteness is the first. Socially astute individuals comprehend what's going on during social interactions. You might consider this being socially aware and sensitive to others' interests. Interpersonal influence is the second. Individuals who wield interpersonal influence are subtle and convincing in their style, and they do this by being adaptive in their use of tactics. Next is networking ability. People with this skill know how to build and rely on a diverse and extensive network of people. They have many relationships that help them collect information and get things done. And finally, apparent sincerity. This dimension of political skill involves the credibility of the individual, how much she appears to be genuine and authentic and to have integrity.

Let's look at two of these dimensions in greater detail, social astuteness and apparent sincerity. Research by Ferris and colleagues suggest that social astuteness is particularly important as an overall skill. People who are high on this dimension are rated by supervisors as having better job performance, and this is likely, both because they're able to work effectively with others, and because they're good at making sure their bosses see them performing well.

So why does this skill matter? Well, let's consider what happens when a well-intentioned employee tries to use a soft tactic but fails, because he's not socially astute. Imagine an employee dressed up, walking into a meeting with his boss. The meeting is very tense because there are some serious issues on the table. His boss is concentrating and working hard to control his temper in this conversation. Our socially inept employee makes a joke in the middle of the meeting. Oh it's a good thing you are such a handsome guy or I might be intimidated by all this serious talk. This is an example of a poorly placed and poorly executed ingratiation attempt. Almost certainly, it will result in the boss being even more frustrated.

Can you get better at being socially astute? A book by Stanford Business Professor Jeffrey Pfeffer, appropriately called *Power,* concludes with a chapter called, "It's Easier Than You Think." He's talking about gaining power and political skill, and basically suggests that you should learn what the research says, such as by reading his book, of course, but also by taking a course like this and then applying that information in your everyday work. Specifically with regard to being socially astute, the key is to practice paying attention to what people are doing and saying. Become an observer, and follow up with people by asking lots of questions. See if you can become better at discerning when people are excited and when they're nervous, which can look alike. See if you can figure out when they're open to new ideas, or when maybe they're too overwhelmed.

Let's move to another dimension of political skill, apparent sincerity. The idea is that some people are seen in ways that make them seem genuine and believable, and they're likely to have much success with any influence effort. This idea has been defined and described many ways, and no one way is correct. Let's use the principle set down by Sandy Allgeier in her book *The Personal Credibility Factor*. Allgeier offers very straightforward advice for how to be credible. She suggests seven steps.

Know your stuff. Take the time to learn what you need to know. The connection to informal informational power is clear here, but this is also about knowing how to do your job well, whatever it is. You cannot overlook the very basic issue of being capable of doing what is expected of you. Allgeier goes on. Keep all commitments. Continuing with the idea that you need to meet expectations about your work, you should always follow through. If you say you're going to do something, just do it. Allgeier includes in this list honoring confidences and avoiding gossip. If you promise not to say anything, keep that promise. If you find out interesting information, don't go spreading it unless you have confirmed it and no one is hurt by you doing it.

Allgeier's list continues with know yourself, the good and the bad. Show a little humility and recognize that you do have weaknesses as well as strengths. This is related to referent power, as you're unlikely to be respected if you're an arrogant jerk. Allgeier includes, choose to value something in others. Show concern and empathy for other people, finding something to appreciate and like in them. This is a good path to building relationships with anyone. Next, ask more questions and listen. The best way to learn and to show interest in others is to ask questions, so ask away. The last tip from Allgeier's book is perhaps considered to be a combination of the above. It suggests, above all, that you should seek to take conversations you have with other people seriously. Take the time to really listen and get to know people.

Earlier in this lecture I asked you to recall your most and least favorite colleague. Return to the images of their faces in your mind right now. With your favorite colleague, I imagine that you have had multiple credible interactions. When you conversed, was there direct and honest agreements, or maybe even disagreement? Was there eye contact and at least some mutual interest? I imagine this was true, and these were exactly what was missing from your interactions with your least favorite colleagues.

To wrap up, political skill enables one to find the best time to use particular tactics and to then execute them appropriately. Taken together, power and political skill are critical factors that determine the success of influence. Influential people at work develop their power bases and their political skill, and they're deliberate in their selection of tactics that match them.

As we near the end of our lecture, let's discuss two things you can try. First, work to develop your referent power. Referent power is about a relationship you have with others based on respect and admiration. How can you get people to respect you if they don't already? Picking up on Allgeier's tips, I want to encourage you to initiate conversations with people you hope to influence in the future. Take the long-term view. Get to know them as well as you can, their interests, values, and personal history. It may sound silly if you haven't tried it, but simply by listening, you'll be establishing a relationship that's based on respect, and that will help you in the future.

For the second thing to try, I want you to make a plan. I want you to make a very concrete plan to improve your credibility with a specific person. To make it specific, consider a particular relationship, maybe your spouse, or a colleague at work, or your kids, and ask yourself, what specific steps can I take to improve my credibility with this person? The key here is to be specific; to say, I'm going to keep all my commitments is just regurgitating Allgeier's list items. You need a more specific plan. How and when will you ask more questions? How and when will you keep your commitments? Consider that one way to make all your commitments is to make fewer of them and be more realistic. So perhaps you should consider not making any commitments or promises unless you take the time to write it down.

We've arrived at the end of our second lecture on influence tactics. This is the second T in the ATTiC model, and it's time to move on to the final letter of our acronym, C for context. In the next lecture we'll talk about powerful context characteristics that can have an impact on our attempts to influence other people.

How Context Shapes Influence
Lecture 7

Human beings are perceptive and social by nature; we constantly observe and interpret what those around us are doing, often without even being aware of it. In trying to make sense of our uncertain environment, we also frequently use the behavior of others as a guide. Of course, if you're aware of these tendencies, you can use that knowledge to your advantage in a moment of influence. In this lecture, we will look at the last element of the ATTiC model, context. We'll discuss three contextual cues identified by author Bob Cialdini to which people naturally respond: scarcity, authority, and social proof. When present, these cues dramatically affect how likely people are to be influenced.

Scarcity

- In many situations, people do not know the actual worth of an object or action. If you're asked to purchase a new smart phone with unique features for $500, you would not immediately know whether the phone is worth $500. One way you might determine whether this is a good deal is by looking at the context: How many of the phones are available? Is there competition for them? If there are only a few phones and everyone seems to want one, then the phone is scarce. And a mental shortcut we all use is that scarce goods are more valuable. Thus, if a particular context creates scarcity, it cues us into action.

- We can see the effects of scarcity in auctions for unique items, such as movie memorabilia or the work of famous artists, and in more mundane situations, such as the Black Friday sales on the day after Thanksgiving. Often, the same goods that are on sale on Black Friday are available for a similar price on the day before and the day after, but retailers take advantage of our natural instincts to value the scarce to get us moving.

- A similar mechanism operates when a school district or watchdog group "bans" an item; interest is raised on the part of the public. Such an action also sends a signal that the supply of the item may become restricted, and thus, the item will become more valuable. For example, when the Vatican condemned Sister Margaret A. Farley's 2006 book *Just Love: A Framework for Christian Sexual Ethics*, the book quickly rose from number 142,982 on Amazon's overall sales ranking to number 16.

By understanding and using contextual cues, such as scarcity, savvy marketers can influence us to buy.

- The scholar James Chowning Davies has put forth a theory of political revolution suggesting that scarcity plays an important role here, as well. Davies examined high-profile political revolutions in Russia, Egypt, and the United States and developed what he called the "J curve" of revolution.

  o This occurs following prolonged progress in acquiring freedoms and goods, when a reversal creates a gap between expectations and reality. On a plot of growth in freedoms and goods over time, there would be a sudden dip, and the plot would resemble an upside-down letter *J*.

  o What happens following the dip can be considered in terms of scarcity in that as freedoms become increasingly available, there are commensurate increases in optimism and hope. But when there is a reversal, people begin to feel that those freedoms are threatened and, potentially, scarce. The fear of further reversals and even fewer freedoms in the future may be one of the forces that pushes people to raise arms and revolt, that is, to fight to secure what suddenly feels scarce.

Authority

- In the 1960s, Stanley Milgram conducted his now well-known research into how far people would go to comply with orders.

  o In Milgram's experiment, a research participant was asked to play the role of teacher in helping another participant memorize pairs of words. When the learner (a research confederate) made a mistake in recalling the correct word, the teacher was instructed to push a lever that delivered an electric shock as punishment. As the learner made more mistakes, the teacher was instructed to deliver stronger shocks.

  o In reality, there were no shocks, but the learners acted as though there were. If the teacher asked the experimenter whether the shocks should continue, the experimenter would reply with one of four standard prompts. These short statements were the full extent of the continued efforts to influence participants to comply with the request to deliver punishment.

  o The majority of people obeyed the experimenter and continued to administer shocks, even after the learner seemed to become unresponsive. In the original study, 26 people out of 40 (65 percent) went on to administer shocks at a level labeled "450 Volts: Danger: Severe Shock" and beyond when the learner stopped responding.

  o Professor Jerry Burger from Santa Clara University conducted a partial replication of Milgram's experiment in 2009. Burger and his team found that 67 percent of men and 73 percent of women were prepared to continue to administer shocks beyond the 150-volt level.

- Additional studies by Milgram helped to explain why so many people were willing to continue the original experiment. Milgram found that proximity of the learner and of the authority figure (the experimenter) to the subject made a significant difference. Research participants were less willing to fully comply when the learner was nearby and when the authority figure was remote.

- In his more recent experiment, Professor Burger tested another condition: having someone else in the room who modeled refusal.
  o This other person was also a confederate, but the research participant was told that this person would be a teacher in future rounds. As the shocks increased in intensity, the confederate would first say, "I don't know about this," followed by, "I don't think I can do this." The confederate said nothing else and did not make eye contact with the participant.

  o The rates of compliance for moving beyond 150 volts decreased slightly (55 percent for men and 68 percent for women), but the difference is not large enough to be statistically significant with the sample size used. Thus, even with one person modeling resistance, more than half of the participants in Burger's experiment were willing to follow orders and put another person in pain.

  o Clearly, a context that includes an authority figure is one that is highly prone to elicit compliance.

- Would it be easy for a manager to convince a subordinate to fake investment records or to inflate a quarterly earnings report by postdating a financial transaction? Given the results of Milgram's and Burger's experiments, it seems not only possible but likely that the average employee would comply. We would like to think that we have the strength of character to refuse, but research suggests otherwise. We use the authority of the person giving orders as an excuse to believe that we do not have personal responsibility.

- And therein lies the secret to helping reduce the power of authority: If people are told that they will be held personally responsible for their actions, they should be substantially less likely to succumb to pressure from an authority figure.

Social Proof

- In another experiment, Milgram had five research confederates stop and look up at a building on 42nd Street in New York City. He found that approximately 80 percent of people passing by also looked up. His results confirm that we all often make sense of the world around us by watching for cues from other people.

- Social proof came into the news in 1964 in the famous case of Catherine Genovese. Although 38 people heard Genovese's screams as she was being attacked in the street by an assailant with a knife, no one called the police. The incident sparked public outrage, as well as a host of research studies.

  o In one of these studies, social psychologists Bibb Latané and John Darley sought to learn why no one helped Genovese. They asked a research confederate to slump over and appear to be passed out on a busy street or to feign an epileptic seizure.

  o The researchers found that when the seizure occurred in front of a single person, that person would help 85 percent of the time. When it occurred in front of five people, help came only 31 percent of the time.

  o This is the essence of social proof: If no one else is helping, people think that they shouldn't help either. Interestingly, studies also show that once one person steps in, others quickly follow.

- In his book on influence, Bob Cialdini reviews this evidence and offers good advice for ensuring that you get aid if you are in trouble in a crowd. Cialdini advises that you reduce all uncertainty by identifying a specific person in the crowd and asking for help. Once that person helps, others will follow, but to get the first person to move, you need to make sure he or she has a sense of personal responsibility.

- Advertisers use social proof extensively with such claims as "four out of five dentists" choose a particular brand of toothpaste or "10 million customers can't be wrong." Bartenders and church ushers use social proof by salting their tip jars and collection plates. In this way, social proof can be used to draw people to new products, services, and ideas.

- As Cialdini notes, social proof, like scarcity and authority, involves quick psychological processes that operate outside of our control. These processes are, in effect, shortcuts that our brains use to make sense of the social world and to make decisions. But these instantaneous processes can be used against us by unscrupulous people who lie about their authority or falsify numbers to establish social proof.

Application: Understanding Context
- To further explore the power of context, sit in public and watch people waiting in line at a store. Consider the level of conformity and the forces that create it. How many people don't seem to mimic others? How many seem willing to break out of the box and not follow what others are doing?

- To apply the scarcity tactic, try making yourself "scarce" when it comes to buying. The next time you are looking to buy a car, reach out via e-mail or the web to a few dealers. Find out if they have the car you'd like in stock and what deal you could get. Then visit the dealership where you would prefer to buy. Let the salesperson know that you have heard from three other dealers who are interested in your business. In this way, you are arguing that your business and your time are scarce. A salesperson who wants the sale should move at this point to make an offer that appeals to you!

Suggested Reading

Burger, "Replicating Milgram."

Latané and Darley, *The Unresponsive Bystander.*

Milgram, *Obedience to Authority.*

1. Watch people waiting in line at a store. Consider the level of conformity and the forces that create it. What percentage of people don't seem to mimic others?

2. Do something to make yourself "scarce" in your next significant purchasing decision. For example, the next time you are looking to buy a car, contact a few dealers by e-mail to learn what they might offer you. Then, visit the dealership where you would prefer to buy. Tell the salesperson, "I would like to buy from you, but I don't have much time and I have prices from three other dealers. What is the best offer you can make me?" A salesperson who wants the sale should recognize that your time is scarce and move to make an offer that appeals to you!

How Context Shapes Influence
Lecture 7—Transcript

Stand in the middle of a crowd and yawn. Watch what happens around you. Cough to draw a little attention to yourself, and then look sharply to your left. Again, watch what happens around you. Even more telling, take four friends, go outside to where there's a busy street. All of you stop at the same time and look up to an empty window. What do you think will happen? American social psychologist Stanley Milgram worked with his colleagues to test precisely what happened in this situation. He asked groups of research confederates to stop on a busy street and look up at a building even though there was nothing there. This was a busy New York City street. He varied the size of the group, sometimes from one person to two or three, up to actually 15 people. The experimenters, they got to watch, and they counted the percent of people walking by who also looked up at the building. When only one research confederate stopped and looked, 40 percent of the people walking by looked. With two, the percent went up to nearly 60 percent. Beginning with five and going up in group size, nearly 80 percent of the passersby looked.

Human beings are perceptive and social by nature, so we're constantly looking around and interpreting what those around us are doing, often without even being aware that we're doing it. We're also constantly trying to make sense of a confusing and uncertain world, and we use the behavior of others as a frequent guide. A yawn, for example, is quite contagious. Scientists aren't completely sure why, but the evidence is clear that upon seeing another person yawn, you're much more likely to yawn yourself. More often than not, responses like this occur in a click-whirr fashion. They happen quickly. They're not controlled by any deliberate thought or planning. Yawning, looking up in the sky, blinking your eyes, folding your arms. People around us often influence our behavior outside of our awareness, and we naturally and unthinkingly mimic what they do. Of course, if you're aware that this happens, you can better understand yourself and others and in a moment of influence use that knowledge to your advantage.

In this lecture, we will visit the context corner of the ATTiC model. We'll discuss three contextual cues to which people naturally respond. When present, these cues dramatically affect how people are likely to be influenced. We'll use language crafted by, Bob Cialdini, author of the bestselling book *Influence: Science and Practice*. Cialdini refers to these three cues as scarcity, authority, and social proof. Let's begin with scarcity.

In many situations, people do not know the actual worth of an object or an action, so if you're asked to purchase a brand new smart phone with features unlike anything on any other phone on the market, for $500, you would not immediately know whether the phone is actually worth $500. Should you buy it? How do you figure out whether that's a good deal? One way that people do this is by looking at the context. How many of these phones are available? Is there a competition among people for them? Is there a line forming? If there are only a few phones and everyone seems to want one, then the phone is scarce, and a mental shortcut we all use is that scarce goods must be more valuable. So if a particular context creates scarcity, it cues us into action.

Witness what happens in a live auction. On the block is a single, white polyester suit. It garners attention, and two people keep raising their hands to outbid the other. Looking at each other, sizing each other up, they continue to raise their bids. In the end, the polyester suit sells for $145,000. Sounds like an unlikely scenario, right? Well, it really happened. The white suit in question was the one worn by John Travolta in *Saturday Night Fever*, and though $145,000 is a lot to pay for a dated piece of clothing, it was one of a kind. It was the one Travolta wore during filming, and the competition between bidders drove up the price. In describing this bidding contest in his book, Cialdini reported that the auctioneer was delighted and quite politic when describing the outcome. He simply noted, "That certainly is a record for polyester."

Of course, that's not a record for an auction. Many individuals and companies opt to sell their goods and possessions at auctions. As long as they can get a good crowd there, then they can get competition. At Sotheby's art auctions, there are often multimillion dollar prices on certain items. A piece by the American abstract artist Jackson Pollock, for example, fetched over $40 million. Not everyone is a fan of Pollock's unusual drip style of painting, but there are enough fans of his unique work and not enough original paintings to go around. Especially because Pollock died in a car crash at the age of 44.

For most of us, Sotheby's auctions are a bit outside of our price range, but we can witness more mundane examples of scarcity in the Black Friday sales that happen just after, well, now, in some cases, on Thanksgiving. With only a few items at sale prices, lines often form in advance, and people work hard to get those items, resorting at times to pushing, shoving, and name calling. Often the same goods are available the day before and the day after for a price that really isn't that much different. But retailers take advantage of our natural instincts to value the scarce to get us moving. If a particular item is tagged limited availability it must be valuable. Right? This is when retailers, knowing how we interpret scarcity, turn this context into an influence tactic, and they get us to buy. By understanding and using contextual cues, like scarcity, savvy marketers keep finding new ways to make us buy, buy, buy. A similar mechanism operates when a movie or book is banned. When a school district or watchdog group bans a particular item, it raises interest on the part of the public. It also sends a signal that this item may become restricted in supply, and thus more valuable.

For example, the Vatican condemned Sister Margaret A. Farley's 2006 book *Just Love: A Frame Work for Christian Sexual Ethics*. In her book, Farley wrote about human sexuality, gay marriage, and even masturbation. It was considered blasphemous by the Roman Catholic Church. After the ban, concerns were raised about how easy it would be to get a copy. The book quickly rose from number 142,982 on Amazon's overall sales ranking to number 16. It also became the number one best selling religious studies book for some time. Some of you might think that this is all about the racy title and the subject, but remember, the book had been out for some time, and sales had been mediocre. The spike in sales occurred after the ban. This has led some to call book banning the new Oprah effect, named after the boost in book sales that occurs when Oprah Winfrey selects a book for her reading club. Making something scarce can be just as powerful as an endorsement.

There's another interesting angle to scarcity. The scholar James Chowning Davies has put forth a theory of political revolution that suggests scarcity plays an important role. Davies examined high-profile political revolutions in

Russia, Egypt, and the United States and developed what he calls the J curve of revolution. This is when, following prolonged progress in the ability of citizens to acquire freedoms and goods, there's a reversal that creates a gap between expectations and reality. If you were plotting growth in freedoms and goods over time, there's a sudden dip, so it looks like the upside down letter J.

What happens following the dip can be considered in terms of scarcity, and that as freedoms become increasingly available, there are commensurate increases in optimism and hope. But with a reversal, those freedoms begin to feel threatened and potentially scarce. The fear of further reversals and even fewer freedoms in the future may be one of the forces that pushes people to come together, to raise arms and revolt, to fight to secure what suddenly feels scarce. So our first context cue that affects influence is scarcity. When something appears scarce it seems more valuable and people will act on it much as if its objective value was very high.

Let's move on to discuss authority. At the top of this lecture I mentioned the experiment Stanley Milgram conducted on the New York City sidewalks. In the 1960s, Milgram took the question of conformity and compliance even further. Given what had happened in Nazi Germany in the years before and during World War II, he wondered just how far people would go to comply with orders. He created an experiment, now very well known, where a research participant is asked by the experimenter to punish someone else with electrical shocks. How many people would comply? How many people would comply if the shocks were increased to nearly deadly levels? Let's talk about the experiment first, and then we'll talk about what Milgram and his students found.

Upon arriving at the lab, a research participant would meet up with another person, and they would draw straws to see who plays the role of teacher and who plays the role of learner. In reality, the participant always ended up being the teacher, and the other person, the learner, was always a research confederate. The participant was asked to help the learner, this is the confederate actor, memorize pairs of words. When the learner made a mistake recalling the correct word, the teacher was instructed to push a lever that delivered an electrical shock as punishment. As the learner made more mistakes, the teacher was instructed to deliver stronger and stronger shocks. The confederate would always make mistakes, as planned by the experimenter, so the research participant was asked, in each experiment, to deliver increasingly powerful shocks.

In reality, there were no shocks, but the learners were trained actors. They acted quite convincingly as though the shocks were real, and as the shocks got more intense, the learner would begin to complain. Sometimes the participant would look at the experimenter and ask, "Should I go on?" When this happened, the experimenter would prod the subject to continue using one of four standard prompts: Please continue; The experiment requires you to continue; It is absolutely essential that you continue; and, You have no other choice you must go on. These statements were the full extent of the continued efforts to influence participants to comply with the request to deliver punishment.

What sort of things did the actor playing the learner say? It began with, "ow," and as the intensity increased moved to actual screams of pain. The learner would eventually say, "I'm no longer in the experiment! Let me out." How many participants continued to shock the learner even after he asked to have it stop? What about after the learner didn't say anything at all to the teacher's questions and only groaned in pain with the next shock? Most people were, and to this day continue to be, surprised by the results. The majority of people, the majority, obeyed the experimenter and continued to administer shocks even after the learner became unresponsive. In the original study, this was 26 out of 40, 65 percent, who went on to administer shocks at a level that was labeled on the machine 450 volts. Danger: Severe shock.

When I present these results to students today, many of them say, "I'd never do that." or, "That would never happen today." Fortunately, Professor Jerry Burger from Santa Clara University took pains to replicate Milgram's experiment. And we now know how much people have changed since the 1960s. We're certainly wearing different clothes, but let's talk about the study. In a study published in 2009, Burger and his team report a partial replication of Milgram's study. To address ethical concerns that we're very sensitive to now, a clinical psychologist was employed to screen students for anxiety and depression. To be cautious, 38 percent of the students who were signed up for this experiment were dropped from the study before going further.

Burger ran the experiment with 29 men and 41 women. And it included students, but it included some older adults too. They ranged in age from 20 to 81; the average age was 42. The subjects varied in education level as well. In addition to the college students, there were some that only had high school, and there were some with Master's degrees. The experiment used the exact same script from Milgram's original work, but Burger made a few changes. He was quicker to stop the experiment and would do so if the subject refused to continue after the four standard experimental prompts had all been used, or if the subject made a decision to proceed beyond the 150-volt level.

So what did Burger find? Of the men, 67 percent were prepared to continue beyond the 150-volt level. Of the women, 73 percent were prepared to continue. So much for the idea that women are always more compassionate than men. Because of Burger's more cautious experimental setup, the results here are a bit more conservative in their estimation of obedience. And some scientists have interpreted this data to mean that people today are more willing to go against authority, but even those critics admit that context continues to be an important and powerful predictor of behavior.

Why would so many people be willing to continue the experiment? Further studies by Milgram, who conducted his research at Yale University, helped to describe why. Remember that Milgram's basic experimental setup involves three people, the teacher, who is the actual research participant; the learner, who's actually a confederate pretending to be a volunteer; and the experimenter, who serves as an authority figure. In his further studies, Milgram examined proximity of the learner to the subject. Is there just the voice because the person is in the other room? Is there some visual contact, or are they in the same room actually touching each other? And the proximity of the authority figure, is the authority figure, the experimenter, present all the time, or does this person leave the room?

Proximity made a big difference in both cases. Research participants were less willing to fully comply when a learner was near them and when the authority figure was remote, so being closer to the person you would be doing harm to and being further away from the authority figure asking you to do harm led people to stop sooner. Perhaps it was being at Yale University, an Ivy League institution, that might convey extraordinary levels of authority, and that's what pushed people to continue. To test this idea, Milgram moved the experiment to nearby Bridgeport, Connecticut and called the study team the Research Associates of Bridgeport, an organization name that was just created for the study.

The building used was a somewhat rundown commercial building, and the lab was clean, but sparsely furnished, and there, the experiment was replicated. Milgram concluded that there was no real difference between obedience levels from Yale University to this other setting. However, the number of people who administered maximum shocks at Bridgeport was 48 percent versus 65 percent at Yale. Knowing what we know today about sample sizes and confidence intervals, it's certainly possible that this change made more of a difference than Milgram concluded. At the time, Milgram seemed genuinely surprised that so many people continued to obey, so he emphasized the high levels of obedience in Bridgeport. These classic results generally support the idea that many people will comply with authority figures, even when it goes against their own judgment. This effect is diminished when the authority figure is further removed or when the consequences of their action are much more visible to them.

In his more recent experiment, Professor Burger tested another condition, having someone else in the room who modeled refusing the authority figure's request. This other person was also a research confederate, but the participant was told that this person was going to be a teacher in future rounds. As the shocks increased in intensity this person would say, "I don't know about this," and then, "I don't think I can do this." The confederate said nothing else, and did not, by the script of the experiment, ever make eye contact with the participant, so this amounted to two short sentences. Did it make a difference? Not really. The rates of compliance for moving beyond or being willing to move beyond 150 volts were down a little, 55 percent for men and 68 percent for women, but the difference is not large enough to be statistically significant with this sample size. So even with one person there modeling resistance to authority, more than half the participants in Professor

Burger's more recent experiment were willing to follow orders, and because they were asked, put another person in pain.

Clearly, a context that includes an authority figure is one that is highly prone to elicit compliance. Let's extrapolate these findings to a context where there's no identifiable victim and the authority figure is literally standing over someone's shoulder. Would it be easy for a manager visiting a subordinate's office to stand over his shoulder and look at his spreadsheet and convince him to fake or modify investment records or to maybe just inflate a quarterly earnings report by postdating a particular financial transaction? Given professors Milgram's and Burger's results, it seems not only possible, it seems likely that the average employee would comply. While some people will have the strength of character to hold true to what they believe is correct, and all of us would like to think we wouldn't be the one to make those changes or fake the data, research suggests that the majority of us would comply. We might not like it, but we use the authority of the person giving orders as an excuse to help ourselves believe we do not have personal responsibility.

And therein lies the secret to helping reduce the power of authority. If people are told that they will be personally responsible for their actions, they should be substantially less likely to succumb to pressure from an authority figure. If you want to push yourself to go against authority, remind yourself that at the end of the day you will be ultimately responsible for what you do. In other words, before you comply with a request from an authority figure, ask yourself: am I comfortable having others know that I did this? Some people, including the famous investor and philanthropist Warren Buffett, refer to this as the newspaper test. How would you feel if there was story about what you just did on the front page of the local newspaper? Would you be ashamed if people knew? If so, then you should stop and think again before complying.

So far we've talked about scarcity and authority as contextual cues that facilitate influence. Now we move to our third and final cue for this lecture, social proof. Under conditions of uncertainty, we look around us and use other people's actions to guide us. Recall the study mentioned at the opening of this lecture. Professor Milgram, leaving behind his fake shock machine, took his confederates into the street. When five of his confederates stopped on a busy street and looked up at a building, approximately 80 percent of the people passing by also looked up. Milgram did this study on 42nd Street in New York City, and there is no reason to expect it wouldn't happen in any crowded area near where you live. People are people, and they pay attention and make sense of the world around them by watching for cues from other people.

Social proof can result in some terrible things happening. A famous case in New York City revealed that sometimes people will stand idly by as something terrible happens. In the early morning hours of March 13, 1964, Catherine Genovese was walking home in Queens, New York, when she was attacked by an assailant with a knife. Subsequent news reports wrote that 38 people heard her screams that night, yet no one called the police. Why did no one call? Is it because people living in the city are apathetic or cruel? The incident and the media coverage that followed sparked lots of dialogue and a host of research studies.

In one of these studies, social psychologists Bibb Latané and John Darley sought to find the reasons why people did not help Genovese. They asked a research confederate to slump over and appear passed out on a busy street. Many people just walked by. In another one of their studies, they had a confederate appear to have an epileptic seizure. When it occurred in front of a single person, that person would help 85 percent of the time. When it happened in front of five people, help would only come 31 percent of the time. There is clearly no safety in numbers. If everyone is looking to see if others will help, and everyone fails to act, that's social proof. No one else is helping, so I probably should not help. In these studies a funny thing happens once one person starts to help. It only takes one person to step in, and then social proof kicks in and others quickly follow.

Like Milgram, Latané, and Darley were also working in the streets of New York City. Perhaps Canadians are nicer than New Yorkers. A study conducted in Toronto by professor Abraham Ross found that single bystanders who saw smoke in a room billowing from a door nearby reported it 90 percent of the time, but again, he was working in Canada. When two passersby were present, now research confederates were asked to ignore the smoke and not say anything, only 16 percent of the time did someone speak up, only 16 percent of the time. Ninety percent versus 16 percent, even in Canada, this is the power of social proof.

In his book on influence, Bob Cialdini reviews this evidence and offers fantastic advice about how to get aid if you are in trouble in a crowd. To be sure that you get the help you need, Cialdini advises that you reduce all uncertainty and pick a person in the crowd pointing and saying, "You, sir, in the blue jacket. I need help; call an ambulance." Once that person who's been picked out and held accountable steps in to help, social proof will kick in, and others will follow. But to get the one person you need to move, you do need to create for that person a sense of personal responsibility.

So far we've discussed social proof as it relates to harsh realities of people not providing help if no one else is helping. And it's easy to see social proof and authority operating in cults, where people join and stay with groups that have esoteric and even strange beliefs. But how could social proof be used more positively to get someone to do something? Advertisers use it extensively with ads saying, four out of five dentists, or nine out of 10 people, or by claiming that 10 million customers can't be wrong. Bartenders and church greeters use social proof by salting their tip jars and collection plates. If other people are giving, people will reason, then I should give too. So social proof can be used to draw people to new products, new services, and new ideas, such as when a video posted online begins to draw a crowd with many views. When that starts to happen, even more people will click to watch.

Cialdini raises an important concern, which is that social proof, like scarcity and authority, involves quick psychological processes that operate outside of our mental control. They are, in effect, shortcuts that our brain uses to make sense of our social world and make what generally are quite good decisions. But these instantaneous processes can be used against us by unscrupulous people who lie about their authority, or makeup numbers to make us believe that social proof is there. We should condemn these practices in the strongest terms, because they use our own brains against us. There's nothing ethical about manipulating social proof. Sales people and other influence artists should make the sale on the strength of the arguments in their products, not on tricks, ploys, or lies.

In this lecture, we have discussed three context features that have strong effects on influence: scarcity, authority, and social proof. Although each can occur naturally, the examples used in this lecture should make it clear that agents sometimes alter contexts as a way to improve their chances of successful influence. Whether they occur as context or tactic, it's helpful for you to understand how these may be affecting your decisions and behavior outside of your awareness. To help you explore these ideas further, let me propose two activities that can help you better understand the power that context has over us all.

First, sit in public and watch people waiting in line at a store. Watch their behavior and consider the level of conformity and the forces that create it. What percent of people do you notice who don't mimic others? What percent seem willing to break outside the lines and not follow what others are doing? What percent are doing exactly what the people around them are doing? Take a look.

The second thing I would encourage you to try is to apply the scarcity tactic the next time you are going to buy a big ticket item. The next time you're looking to buy a car, for example, do a lot of research. Reach out via the e-mail, your e-mail account or the web, to a few different car dealers. Find out if they have what you'd like to buy in stock and find out what kind of deal you could get. Then visit the dealership where you would really prefer to buy, get to know the sales person. When the sales person moves in for the close, you could simply say, "I would like to buy from you, but I've already heard from three other dealers who are interested in my business. I only have so much time to continue to look into who can offer the best deal. What is your best offer that you can make to me today?" At this point you've argued that your business, your time, is scarce. A salesperson who wants the sale should move at this point to make you an offer that will appeal.

In this lecture we've finished our tour of the ATTiC model, starting with agent and, here, ending with context. In the next lecture we'll take up more specific applications of influence, beginning with impression management that occurs in many work settings, like the employment interview. If you've always wondered about the best way to ace an interview, then join me for the next lecture to find out.

Practicing Impression Management
Lecture 8

A corporate brand is more than just a product or logo; it is an idea that distinguishes one product or service from others. Interestingly, people can also have brands. Some people, because of careful attention to the impressions they make on others, have developed positive images that can work to their advantage in many situations. When we discuss brands in this way, they are not really distinct from the idea of reputation or image. What is useful to understand is that the techniques that companies use to build their brands can also be applied by individuals. In this lecture, we'll talk about active efforts to manage impressions, a topic that comes up frequently in business contexts.

Shaping Your Impression

- The term "impression management" refers to tactics people use to establish particular images or reputations. There is some overlap here with influence tactics, but the nature of the influence here is distinct. With impression management, you are generally trying to influence someone to believe that you are a good person or, in the context of a job interview, a good employee. That is, you are trying to create a "good impression" that can work to your advantage later.

- Most generally, impression management tactics can be self-focused (self-promoting) and other-focused (ingratiating). These two broad approaches have been studied in interview and workplace contexts.

- In a study conducted by Cornell's Tim Judge and Bob Bretz, graduates from two large universities, one on the East Coast and one in the Midwest, were asked to complete a survey about how they generally influence others at work and about their career outcomes, including current salary and number of promotions.
  - Controlling for other potential causes of career success, the researchers found that those who focused on job performance

had lower salaries and fewer promotions than those who focused on their supervisors.

o   Perhaps the greatest lesson from this particular study is that it is better to make your boss feel good than to make yourself look good, at least when it comes to getting your next promotion.

A Firm Handshake

- Impression management is particularly important in a job interview. In this situation, you have to meet your interviewer, answer some questions, and have the interviewer walk away saying, "That's the candidate we should hire!" How do you convince the interviewer to come to that conclusion?

The signals of competence and warmth sent by a strong handshake probably connect with people at a primitive level.

- Research suggests that the handshake at the beginning of an interview can make a significant difference in the outcome.

  o   In one study conducted at the University of Iowa, Professor Greg Stewart and his colleagues and students explored the question of whether their handshakes helped undergraduates make a good impression.

  o   Stewart and his colleagues offered a free mock interview service for students, during which the students were greeted by, and shook hands with, five research assistants. The assistants then rated the handshakes on several factors. The ratings by the five assistants were highly correlated, providing a good indication that the ratings were a reliable measure of "handshake ability."

o The professional recruiter who conducted the interviews was not asked about the handshakes but rated each participant on his or her desirability for hire. The recruiter's ratings correlated highly with the handshake ability index. In fact, the quality of the handshake mattered more than any other variable analyzed in the study.

- A good handshake likely conveys two important messages: competence as a professional ("I am confident and strong") and positive feelings toward the recipient ("I am genuinely pleased to meet you"). These messages fit quite well with other research on person perception.
  o For example, Susan Fiske, a professor of psychology at Princeton University, has worked with colleagues to show that people generally pick up on two cues when they first meet someone: competence and warmth (or caring).

  o In a hiring situation, these signals translate to: "I am the kind of person who can get things done, and I can help you because I care about you." We tend to like and trust people who convey those messages and, as a result, are primed to be influenced by them.

Self-Promotion versus Ingratiation
- A 2002 study by Aleks Ellis goes into a bit more detail about the importance of self-promotion and ingratiation in successful job interviews. Ellis divided these two large categories into various specific tactics. For example, ingratiation was broken into opinion conformity and other enhancement.
  o Opinion conformity refers to stating beliefs that one could reasonably assume another person would hold.

  o Other enhancement is more straightforward flattery, that is, saying something positive about another person.

o   In addition, Ellis's study identified a third broad category of impression management tactics: defensive tactics. These include excuses, justifications, and apologies as ways to protect or repair one's reputation.

- Trained assistants in Ellis's study recorded the tactics used by interviewees in structured practice interviews conducted by real employers.
  o   All but 3 out of 119 interviewees used at least one of the impression management tactics: self-promotion, ingratiation, and defensive tactics.

  o   Both self-promotion and ingratiation tactics had a small positive and statistically significant correlation with higher interview evaluations. Defensive tactics had a much lower correlation that was not statistically significant.

  o   Taken as a whole, this study suggests that in formal interview contexts, engaging in both self-promotion and a bit of opinion conformity is likely to create the most positive impression.

Impression Management in Group Efforts

- Researchers Mark Bolino and William Turnley found that different combinations of tactics emerge in situations other than job interviews, such as group projects.

- In their first study, Bolino and Turnley asked 86 college students who had worked on a team project throughout the course of a semester to rate their own use of impression management tactics.
  o   The students were asked to note their use of ingratiation, self-promotion, exemplification (giving the impression of dedication by giving extra effort), supplication (giving the impression of neediness by showing weakness or broadcasting limitations), and intimidation. The students tended to cluster into three profiles with regard to their use of impression management tactics.

- Positives generally made more use of ingratiation, self-promotion, and exemplification, trying to create an overall positive image of themselves. Passives generally made little use of any tactics. Aggressives tended to use all the tactics, both positive and negative.

- Bolino and Turnley also conducted a study in which they asked students to report their use of impression management tactics, rate the desirability of other students as team members, and complete a personality survey.
  - The results of this second study confirmed the three profiles found earlier: positives, aggressives, and passives. It also found that more women were passives (35 percent) than aggressives (21 percent), but more men were aggressives (35 percent) than passives (11 percent).

  - High Machiavellian people were more likely to be either passive or aggressive. Low Machiavellians were more likely to be positive. This finding reinforces the idea that Machiavellian types may actually act differently depending on what they need to accomplish their goals, acting more aggressively when that behavior is allowed and more passively when required.

  - Although the researchers hypothesized that positives would be rated as the best team members, both positives and passives were viewed favorably by other members of their teams. Aggressives were consistently seen as less effective team members.

Impression Management for Executives
- Research offers some insight into both the uses and the effects of ingratiation with CEOs. In one study, Jim Westphal from the University of Michigan and his colleague David Deephouse showed that ingratiation of journalists by CEOs may actually help them get better news coverage.
  - In this study, the researchers sent surveys to executives at four points in time: prior to an earnings announcement, 3 days after, 7 days after, and 30 days after. They then surveyed journalists

who covered these companies at the same intervals. The surveys revealed that CEOs generally used ingratiation in the week following earnings announcements.

o The researchers also learned that journalists wrote fewer negative statements about a firm's leadership and strategy when the CEOs used ingratiation with them. The journalists were more willing to attribute the poor performance of a firm to something other than the firm itself and its leadership, such as the economy.

• In another study, Westphal studied how CEOs can be the victims of ingratiation. Specifically, Westphal found that CEOs who receive flattery from an immediate team are more likely to sustain a losing strategic direction and keep performance poor over longer periods of time.

• It's important to note that ingratiation works best when it is sincere and not directly connected to a particular request.

Application: Making a Good Impression

• Keep track of the number of compliments you give over the course of a week. As you think back over each day, consider how many of those were honest compliments, genuinely meant to share your positive thoughts about others without immediate hope of anything in return. Write down a percentage next to the total number of compliments for each day.

o At the end of the week, revisit these numbers and make a plan for the following week. If you aren't giving at least a few compliments each day, make an effort to be more complimentary of others. And if your percentage of genuineness is low, set a goal to raise it.

o This activity will help you learn to use ingratiation in a way that will build a positive reputation.

- As a second activity, track the number of self-promotional statements you make over the course of a week. As you think back on each day, consider whether you are over- or understating your capabilities. Self-promotion works in many settings, but you can overdo it, which explains why it doesn't always work. If you make more than two or three of self-promoting statements each day, you should begin the next week with the goal of reducing those numbers. Instead of proclaiming your competence, demonstrate it.

Suggested Reading

Bolino and Turnley, "More Than One Way to Make an Impression."

Stewart, Dustin, Barrick, and Darnold, "Exploring the Handshake in Employment Interviews."

Westphal and Deephouse, "Avoiding Bad Press."

Activities to Try

1. Keep track of the number of compliments you give over the course of a week. As you think back over each day, consider how many of those were honest—that is, genuinely meant to share your positive thoughts about others without immediate hope of anything in return. Write down a percentage next to the total number of compliments for each day. At the end of the week, revisit these numbers and make a plan for the next week. If you aren't giving at least a few compliments each day, then make an effort to be more complimentary of others. And if your percentage of genuineness is low, set a goal to raise it.

2. Keep track of the number of self-promotional statements you make over the course of a week. Write down the number of statements, and as you think back on the week, consider whether you are over- or understating your capabilities. Consider ways to demonstrate rather than proclaim your competence.

Practicing Impression Management
Lecture 8—Transcript

When you think of Apple computers, what do you think of? What concepts and ideas come to your head? What about Google? Both of these companies are considered to have well recognized international brands. A brand is much more than just a product or a logo. A brand is an idea that distinguishes one product or service from others. Both Apple and Google brands tend to elicit a common idea. People recognize the logos right away, and the company names themselves seem to bring to mind the concept innovation. The companies recognize this and do all they can to reinforce that connection in consumers' minds, because it helps convince those consumers to buy the next great product coming down the pipe. Think of all the buzz that a new iPhone release generates and even the iPad generated when it first came out. Even with all the jokes about the iPad name, it was talked about incessantly in the media, and people lined up to buy. That was more than just good product design; it was Apple's brand at work.

While many people are familiar with the idea of company brands, it's less often discussed that people can have brands as well. Some people, because of careful attention to the impressions they make on others, have developed a positive image that can work to their advantage time and time again. When we discuss brands in this way, they're not really distinct from the idea of reputation or image. What's useful to understand is that the techniques that companies use to build their brands can also be applied to individuals.

With a little foresight and planning and some discipline in words and action, you can work to create a personal brand that will help you accomplish your personal and professional goals. You might think about it this way; your capacity to influence others begins long before you actually attempt to influence a particular person in a particular setting. It begins with what you do to establish a reputation that allows you to be perceived positively. That positive image will foster liking and trust, which, as we've already discussed, are helpful characteristics of an agent trying to influence a target. In the United States we often discuss Michael Jordan as a classic example of a strong personal brand that has helped a former basketball champion forge a fantastic business career. Oprah Winfrey is no different, nor is Donald Trump, although, for some people, that brand is not as positive as Oprah's.

Let's talk about an example that's less well known in the United States. Let's discuss one of the best brand names in the most populous country in the entire world. In China, the name Li Ning is synonymous with athletic excellence. How did Ning develop this brand? To begin, he was a winner. In the 1982 world cup gymnastic competition he won six of the seven medals awarded for men. Then, in the 1984 summer Olympics held in Los Angeles, he won three gold medals, two silvers, and a bronze. This was the first summer Olympics since 1952 in which the People's Republic of China participated, and he immediately became the most decorated Olympic athlete in Chinese history. He went on to win an astounding 14 world titles in gymnastics. Everything about his accomplishments demonstrates that he is a highly capable athlete. But, in addition, Ning looks like a nice, warm, genuine person. If you look at a picture of Ning, you can immediately see that he has that kind of appeal of someone you would like to know and meet. Because of his image as an outstanding athlete and a nice person, and certainly, to some extent, his timing, Ning became more than just an athlete. He became a symbol of a growing, confident nation. When he retired from gymnastics in 1989, he did something that was quite unusual at the time in China. He leveraged his name and reputation to start his own high-profile sporting goods company, Li Ning Company. It has excelled, opening thousands of stores in China. Indeed, after Ning's high-profile torch lighting in the opening ceremony of the 2008 Beijing Olympics, the company began opening stores around the world. Ning used the association of his name, his brand of athletic excellence, to bring people into stores to buy shoes and sporting apparel. That is the power of a brand, and it speaks to the influence that positive impressions can make on others.

Not all of us can be world-class athletes, but Ning's success brings us to the broad question of how people lay the groundwork for future influence attempts by making good impressions and building a good reputation. If opening a retail store named after yourself was so unusual in China, how was Ning able to convince people that it was a good idea? Research has addressed this question, and we will explore those studies in this lecture. Up to this point in the course, we've been talking about the general processes that underlie successful influence, the components of ATTiC. From this point forward we're going to shift our focus a bit. We're going to move from general processes to specific applications of influence. In this lecture, we'll talk about active efforts to manage impressions, a topic that comes up quite a bit in business contexts.

So let's start the last section of our course with the topic of impression management. How can we shape the perception others have of us so we're more likely to be successful at influencing them in the future? Li Ning has had great success convincing others to buy his athletic apparel. What practical lessons can we learn from this success? And can we apply those lessons when we're on the job or interviewing to get a new job? Impression management refers to tactics that people use to establish a particular impression of themselves. There's some overlap here, obviously, with influence, but the nature of the influence techniques here are a little distinct. With impression management, you're generally trying to influence someone into believing you're a good person, or in the context of a job interview, a good potential employee. That is, you are trying to create a good impression that you can use or work to your advantage later on.

There are quite a few lists of impression-management tactics, but let's start at the broadest level. Most generally, impression-management tactics can be self-focused or other-focused. We'll refer to self-focused tactics as self-promotion, which essentially involves saying, hey, I'm good. Other-focused tactics we'll call ingratiation. Ingratiation involves telling someone else, hey, you're good. These two broad approaches have been studied in contexts where evaluations matter a great deal, interview context, especially, but also in ongoing job contexts.

In our very first lecture, we looked at a study conducted by Tim Judge and Bob Bretz. These two scholars asked graduates from two large universities, one on the East Coast and one in the Midwest to complete a survey about how they generally influence others at work and about their career outcomes, including salary and number of promotions. Controlling for other potential causes of career success, the researchers found that those who focused on job performance actually had lower salaries and fewer promotions than those who focused on their supervisor. So perhaps the greatest lesson from this particular study is that it's better to make your boss feel good than to make yourself look good, at least when it comes to getting that next promotion.

Impression management is particularly important when you are looking for a job. One of the most common hurdles that we all have to jump over is the employment interview. You have to meet someone, shake their hands, answer a few questions, and have that person walk away saying, "Wow. That's someone we should hire." How do you convince that interviewer sitting across the table that you would be a good hire? Here we have to rely on some other research studies. Research suggests that the handshake at the beginning of an interview can make a big difference. Most business people in the United States agree that a good handshake involves a firm, complete grip, eye contact, and vigorous up-and-down movement. How could you design a study to test whether a handshake matters? Well, in one University of Iowa study, Professor Greg Stewart and his colleagues and graduate students examined the handshakes of nearly 100 undergraduate students, and they looked at whether it helped them make a good impression and be recommended for a job. Here's how they did the study.

Stewart and his colleagues offered a free mock interview service for students. Students signed up in advance, were told to come to a designated room, and then when they arrived, they were greeted by a trained research assistant who conducted some introductions, and of course, shook hands. Each participant was then introduced to a few more research assistants as he or she was led to the room where a professional recruiter was waiting. By the end of the session, no fewer than five research assistants had shaken the hand of the participant.

After each greeting, the assistant would excuse him or herself, go into another room, and rate the handshake on the dimensions of firmness of grip, completeness of grip, eye contact, and vigorous up-and-down movement. Now, as it turns out, these dimensions tend to correlate highly, so handshakes offered by participants generally range from overall poor to overall excellent. Just as importantly, the ratings by the five assistants were highly correlated, so we have a good indication that there is a reliable measure for each person of handshake ability.

It's important to note that the professional recruiter who conducted the interviews was never asked about handshakes and was only asked to use the same interview format they use with their job, and then at the end, provide a hiring recommendation. Of course, these interviews always began and ended with a handshake. After each interview, the professional recruiters rated the participant on his or her hireability. Basically, they answered the question, how strongly would you recommend this person to be hired. Guess what related highly to that rating? The handshake ability index. In fact, the quality of the handshake mattered more than any other variable that they collected and analyzed. Clearly, recruiters and potential bosses are taking something away from that first handshake.

But what characteristics can be ascertained from a simple handshake? I can offer my own speculation here. A good handshake likely conveys two things about a person that are very important. First, I'm a competent professional, confident and strong. And second, I like you. I'm looking you in the eye, and I'm genuinely pleased to meet you. If this is, indeed, what a good handshake conveys, then it fits quite well with other research on person perception. For example, Susan Fiske, Professor of Psychology at Princeton University, has worked with a series of colleagues to reveal that people generally pick up on two cues when they first meet someone, competence and warmth. To make this easier to remember, I'll use the terms competent and caring. Competent refers to the ability to get things done; caring refers to being seen as helpful and warm. Think back to our example of Li Ning, as well as to those University of Iowa students who were out there shaking hands.

The signal being sent is a strong one that likely connects with people at a very primitive subconscious level. I am the kind of person who can get things done, and I can help you because I care about you. These are the types of people we like and will trust, and as a result, we're primed and ready to be influenced by them, including buying their products or offering them jobs.

Obviously, a successful interview involves more than just a strong handshake. Impression-management tactics in the interview context have been analyzed in other scholarly studies. For example, a 2002 study by Alex Ellis goes into a bit more detail about the importance of self-promotion and ingratiation in successful job interviews. For starters, Ellis breaks these two large categories into various specific tactics. For example, he breaks ingratiation into two specific tactics, opinion conformity and other enhancement. Opinion conformity refers to stating beliefs that one could reasonably assume the other person would also hold. Other enhancement is more straightforward flattery, saying something positive about that person. In addition, Ellis' study identifies a third broad category of impression-management tactics called defensive tactics. Defensive tactics include excuses, justifications, and even apologies as ways to protect or repair reputation.

Here's how the study worked. The researchers obtained audio tapes of practice interviews conducted by real employers. The interviews were conducted by different recruiters, but all involved the same 14 questions; 119 structured interview audio tapes were coded by two trained research assistants who listened carefully for the use of those tactics. What were the commonly used tactics, and which worked best? Well, first, it's worth noting that all but three of this entire sample of interviewees used at least one of the impression-management tactics, so promotion, ingratiation, and defensive tactics. People were actively trying to manage impressions while answering interview questions.

But, which of those tactics worked? Both self-promotion and ingratiation tactics had a small positive and statistically significant correlation with interview evaluations. So using these tactics was associated with higher evaluations by the interviewer. Defensive tactics, on the other hand, had a much lower correlation that wasn't significant. Taken as a whole, this study suggests that in formal interview context, engaging in both self-promotion and a bit of opinion conformity is likely to create the most positive impression.

Interview situations are quite unique, in that someone is actively making a judgment about you. What happens when people are in a more natural situation, such as working in a group to complete a project? Do people use impression-management tactics in these situations? Do they use them in any particular combination? We might expect to see different combinations of tactics emerge in those types of real-world settings. And in fact, this is exactly what Mark Bolino and William Turnley found in two studies they conducted.

In their first study, Bolino and Turnley took 86 college students who'd been working on an intense course project, working in small teams all semester. They had the students rate their own impression-management tactic use. They had each person note their use of ingratiation, seeking to be likeable by flattering or doing favors; self-promotion, seeking to be viewed as competent by touting abilities and accomplishments; exemplification, seeking to be viewed as dedicated by going above and beyond the call of duty; supplication, seeking to be viewed as needy by showing weakness or broadcasting limitations; and finally, intimidation, seeking to be viewed as intimidating by threatening or bullying others.

People tended to cluster into three profiles with regard to their use of impression-management tactics. Positives generally made use of ingratiation, self-promotion and exemplification, trying to create an overall positive image of themselves. Passives generally made little use of any tactics. And then, there were aggressives; aggressives tend to use all of the tactics, both positive and negative. That means that relative to positives and passives, they're the ones who make greater use of intimidation.

Of course, these patterns don't necessarily tell us whether one profile is better than the other. To address that question, Bolino and Turnley conducted a second study. This time, they surveyed 173 students working in a similar class but in a subsequent semester. The researchers had students report their own use of impression-management tactics and had their team members rate how desirable they were as a team member. In addition, the researchers had everyone complete personality surveys. You may recall from our lecture on the dark triad that there is a negative personality characteristic called Machiavellianism, which is a tendency to do whatever it takes to get one's way. They measured that characteristic.

The results of this second study confirm the pattern of three clusters of people, positives, aggressives, and passives. It also found that more women were passives than aggressives—35 percent versus 21 percent. More men were aggressives—35 percent, as compared to passives, 11 percent. In short, men living up to stereotype were more likely to show up in that aggressive category.

High Machiavellian people were more likely to be either passive or aggressive. Low Machiavellians were more likely to be positive. This finding reinforces the idea that Machiavellian personality types may actually act differently, depending on what they need to accomplish their goals. They'll act aggressive when it's allowed and passive when they think it's required or useful. Among the three profiles, who was perceived as the better team member? Although the researchers hypothesized that positives would always be considered the best team members, both positives and passives were viewed favorably. Aggressives were consistently seen as less effective team members. So if you want to be seen as a good team member, these results provide pretty clear guidance. You should avoid supplication and intimidation and focus on positive impression-management tactics. If you want to pave the way for successful influence down the road, then you can either step back and let other things run, being passive, or you can be positive and use self-promotion and ingratiation, just as you would in an interview setting.

While we've been talking about making a good impression on a team and getting a job, it seems likely that impression-management tactics may play out on bigger stages. What happens, for example, when CEOs who are trying to influence the media and shareholders that all is well and now is the time to buy, buy, buy stock? Well, research offers some insight into how ingratiation plays out in that context.

Jim Westphal from the University of Michigan has actually studied ingratiation and CEOs. In one study he examined how they use ingratiation with reporters. And in a second study he examined how CEOs are affected by others' use of ingratiation on them. In the first study, Westphal and his colleague, David Deephouse, showed that ingratiation of journalists by CEOs, they actually help them get better news coverage for their companies. To show that this occurs, the authors examine relationships between CEOs and journalists using large and midsize public companies. The researchers sent surveys to executives at four points in time, prior to an earnings announcement, three days after that announcement, seven days after, and 30 days after. Then they surveyed journalists who covered these companies at those same time intervals. Using surveys at different points in time helped the researchers understand whether CEOs were generally consistent in how they used ingratiation or whether they popped up in their use ingratiation following negative events. And what they found was that CEOs generally use ingratiation following earnings announcements.

What the researchers were looking for was how journalists would describe the CEO in the firm when an earnings announcement indicates the company failed to meet forecast. And what the researchers found was that journalists wrote fewer negative things about firm's leadership and the firm's strategy when the CEO was using ingratiation on that particular journalist. In other words, CEOs who used ingratiation tended to be let off the hook for bad news by a journalist. In addition, those same journalists went on to be more forgiving of poor performance and to say boy, that's probably the result of the economy rather than of the firm's failure of leadership. So here we see the positive effects of impression-management tactics in big business settings where the use of ingratiation by a CEO can get the company more positive news coverage, something that firms clearly want. From this perspective, CEOs who use ingratiation with journalists are doing their job well. They're using impression management to influence journalists to get good news coverage and to provide cover when there are poor earnings announcements.

But ingratiation doesn't just work as a one-way street. In another study, Westphal worked with colleagues, Park and Stern to explain how CEOs can be the victim of ingratiation. Specifically, Westphal found that CEOs who get lots of flattery from an immediate team are more likely to sustain a losing strategic direction and to keep performance of the company poor over a longer or more extended period of time. This shows that CEOs can fall victim themselves to the impression-management tactics employed by the people around them, and the results aren't good for the company or for the CEOs. Westphal's analysis revealed that those CEOs who were surrounded by flatterers, people using ingratiation, were more likely in the end to lose their job. In short, those CEOs sustained a losing course of action because others were there making them feel good, and they lost their job in the end.

Generally, though, we've seen that ingratiation is an effective tactic that works when you're trying to get a promotion, secure a job in an interview, or build a better image for your company if you're the CEO. I hasten to add, though, that ingratiation can be done poorly, and it can backfire if it's seen as insincere or a blatant attempt at controlling someone. Imagine poorly delivered attempts at ingratiation. The teenage son saying: "Dad, have you lost some weight? Can I borrow the car?" The new employee to her boss: "You are the best manager I've ever had. Can I have a raise?" In both cases it's clear that a compliment is being delivered to get something in return. In these cases the compliment is not perceived as genuine and will not have the desired effect.

Ingratiation works best when it's sincere and not directly and immediately connected to a particular request. If you recall the lecture on influence tactics, I discussed how political skill, especially apparent sincerity, can make the difference between success and failure. This operates with impression management as well. Why does ingratiation work? I believe it works if it believably conveys one of the two most important signals that people want to see before they like and trust another person, that the person is caring. Caring, along with competent, as we discussed, are what you want people to think of you if you want to be influential. While there may be some of us out there who can fake those characteristics well, it is a far easier and far better path to be genuinely competent and genuinely caring.

In this lecture we've moved from the ATTiC model to a specific application of influence, tactics used proactively to make a good impression that will lay the groundwork for influence in the future. But I hope you can see the clear connection between the ATTiC model and impression management. For example, time and time again today we've noted the interaction between the agent and the target. How the agent is perceived by the target is crucial. Is she caring and competent, knowledgeable, admirable? As an agent you can build a reputation that includes these positive descriptors with careful and sincere use of self-promotion, opinion conformity, and ingratiation. In other words, it's in your power to create a personal brand that helps you become more influential.

Let's conclude with two things to try related to impression management. First, keep track of the number of compliments you give over the course of a week. Keep a running tally, and then at the end of each day, write down the total number of compliments. And as you think back over that day, consider how many of those were honest compliments, genuinely meant to share your positive thoughts about others without immediate hope of anything in return. Write a percentage next to the total number of compliments for each day. At the end of the week, revisit those numbers and make a plan for the next week. If you aren't giving at least a few compliments each day, make an effort to be more complimentary. Of course, make sure your compliments are genuine. If your percent of genuineness is low, set a goal to raise it. If you do this, you'll be learning to use ingratiation in a way that will help you build a positive reputation.

As a second activity, track the number of self-promotional statements you make over the course of a week. Write down the number of those statements and think back over the day. Consider whether you are over or understating your capabilities. Self-promotion works in many settings, but you can definitely overdo it, which explains why it doesn't always work. If you have more than just a couple of these statements each day, you should begin the next week with a goal of reducing those numbers. Instead of proclaiming your competence, you should be demonstrating it.

I hope you're feeling better equipped to make a positive impression in any context you might encounter. Next time we'll leave the employment interview and the corporate boardroom behind and head over to the local mall, where we'll discuss influence tactics used by effective sales people.

Selling and Being Sold
Lecture 9

In this lecture, we will focus specifically on sales and service situations to apply some of what we have learned to these all-too-frequent events in our day-to-day lives. What happens in these situations that makes them either fantastic or terrible? As part of this lecture, we will also talk about ways in which you can apply principles of influence to turn the tables on overly pushy sales agents and how can you get a better deal in your sales encounters by applying the concepts learned in this course.

Successful Salespeople
- Successful salespeople are both competent and caring, two fundamental characteristics that have a significant influence on whether or not we trust someone. A good salesperson also behaves in a way that is consistent with Dale Carnegie's classic work *How to Win Friends and Influence People*.

- The core idea behind Carnegie's work is that by changing your own behavior, you can become more confident, better liked, and more persuasive. Among other pieces of advice, Carnegie offered six simple suggestions for how you can get people to like you.
  - First, be genuinely interested in people. For a salesperson, this advice translates into being attentive without being overbearing and asking questions to get to know customers.

  - Second, remember and use peoples' names.

  - Third, be a good listener.

  - Fourth, talk to people in terms of their own interests. A good salesperson focuses the conversation on the customer and his or her needs.

o Fifth, make people feel important and do it sincerely. One of the best ways to do this is to remember a customer's name and other basic facts and use that information to create a genuine personal interaction.

o Finally, use the simple but powerful tool of smiling.

Studies on how servers can increase their tips reveal that repeating an order and smiling broadly yield the greatest increases—100 percent and 140 percent, respectively.

- How does Carnegie's work hold up when studied by hospitality scholars today? A paper by Michael Lynn from Cornell's School of Hotel Administration reviewed a large number of studies on what servers can do to increase their tips. Lynn suggested that the largest increase in restaurant tipping came not from using the customer's name (which yielded a 10 percent increase) but from smiling (which yielded a 140 percent increase).

Emotional Contagion
- Doug Pugh, in a research study published in the *Academy of Management Journal*, suggested two reasons that a positive event, such as a genuine smile, can make people feel better about their encounters with a server or sales agent.
  o First, a smile signifies kindness and builds confidence that you will be helped and get what you seek from the encounter.

o Second, the smile may operate via emotional contagion to put the customer in a good mood. Emotional contagion is exactly what it sounds like: the idea that moods can be transmitted between people. And when put in a good mood, customers are more likely to evaluate the exchange with a server or salesperson more positively.

o Pugh's results support these ideas. He tested bank tellers and found that customers were in better moods and rated their exchanges at the bank more positively when they were served by someone with a smile.

- Of course, not everyone reacts to emotional contagion. If you are particularly deep in a mood state, it may be hard for an outside event to alter your mood. And it might not surprise you to know that people who register high on a psychopath scale are less influenced by the mood states of others and more likely to display an opposite reaction. That's a disturbing idea, but it's consistent with what we learned about the dark triad; it also shows the characteristics of the agent and the target working together to determine the outcome of an influence attempt.

Willing Customers
- In previous lectures, we've noted that some people are more suggestible than others. Are some people more likely to buy following an encounter with a sales agent? Let's look at this question in light of two common pieces of wisdom about shopping: "Don't go to the grocery store when you're hungry," and "Don't buy what you don't need."

- The first of these is a warning not to go shopping when you are likely to think everything looks great. When you are strongly motivated to buy, your pursuit of that goal may lead you to be less rational in considering whether (and what) to buy.
  o When your goal is simply to buy a car, your focus will be on that goal and you may not consider other possibilities, such as walking away and waiting for another day and a better deal.

o We can extend this piece of wisdom about grocery shopping to other situations. If you can, don't wait until your computer crashes or your car stops working to shop for a new one. Start looking in advance, set a budget, and examine the features of the products based on what you need.

- Following the advice not to buy what you don't need can be surprisingly difficult. When you're in a sales situation, try to slow down and fix in your mind that you will not buy at that moment—then walk away. Afterwards, consider the reasons you should and should not buy. This technique may help to displace the commitment that is biasing your thoughts in support of a purchase.

Selling Contexts
- Certain contexts, such as increased incentives, create an even stronger push than usual for sales agents to sell. Perhaps the most famous example of a sales incentive comes from Mary Kay Cosmetics. Representatives who meet certain sales goals receive a car with no lease payment and only a nominal insurance payment.

- Salespeople seem to be most highly motivated by contests with multiple winners. For those who have worked in sales, the logic here is immediately obvious. Competing with 500 other sales agents for one award is much more difficult than competing in a contest in which half the agents can win as long as they hit a particular sales level.
  o The fact that people will work harder if they see a reasonable chance of reward is, in fact, the prediction of one of the most well-established economic theories of human motivation: expected utility theory.

  o Many companies recognize the fact that people will work harder if they believe that the extra effort is likely to yield a meaningful reward; thus, companies offer a range of awards for different levels of sales.

- For customers, the implication here is clear: If you understand the ways in which your sale may help the salesperson, then you may find yourself in a better bargaining position.

Buying a Car

- An article on car buying published in *MSN Money* noted that many of the tips floating around about when and how to bargain for cars are myths. Specifically, you may have read that you should visit a car dealer at the end of the week or the end of the month. But visiting at these times may not be useful if you think about how dealer incentives work.
    - First, there is variability in incentives from dealers; not all of them work on traditional weekly and monthly calendars.

    - Further, a salesperson may already have met a certain threshold; thus, he or she may not really need your sale.

    - Finally, if large numbers of people follow the advice of buying late in the week or month, then sales agents will be busier and feel they have greater leverage to walk away from a reasonable or low-ball offer.

- One of the wisest moves you can make in buying a car is to educate yourself about the incentives that may be in place. Edmunds.com and Kelley Blue Book often have information about incentives from dealers, including when they end. Local dealers may not advertise their incentives, but you can certainly ask.

- Often, the way to get the best deal is simply a matter of economics: Where demand is lowest, companies may establish sales incentives to move inventory. Check for incentives on low-demand cars and find the dealership that has many of these vehicles on the lot.

- Another possibility is to seek out a dealership that does not pay commission on cars. Some dealers put their agents on salary, paying them to be good to customers, not simply to close deals. In his book *To Sell Is Human*, Daniel Pink suggests that the best sales professionals should, in fact, be paid to provide good service, not just to sell.

Reciprocity

- Another important feature of context is reciprocity. If someone has done you a favor recently, you feel a natural obligation to return the favor. The push in our minds to "pay back" is quite powerful.

- Jerry Burger, the professor who replicated the Milgram compliance studies, also studied the power of reciprocity. In a simple experiment involving 120 undergraduate students, he found that when receiving a small favor, 28 percent of participants returned the favor, even though doing so caused them some inconvenience, compared to 5 percent when no favor had been received.

- Because the effect of reciprocity is so powerful, sales agents frequently give away small gifts. To counteract the influence these gifts can have, some hospitals, companies, and government agencies have policies that limit the value and type of gifts that can be given to someone in the organization who has decision-making authority.

- Counteracting reciprocity is difficult because it is a natural psychological process. At a sales party, such as an Amway or Mary Kay party, bringing a small gift for the host might make you feel less compelled to buy.

Application: Leveraging Knowledge of Sales Situations

- In your next service encounter, learn your server's name and use it, ask something personal about the server and use that information, and smile during your encounter. See if your actions change the type of service you receive. If you want to test the effectiveness of this approach, ask for something special that requires some effort and see if you get it.

- The next time you are making a big purchase, make sure to give yourself time. Do an online search for information about features and costs of the product in which you're interested. This research will help you avoid buying something that meets your immediate goal to buy but doesn't give you exactly what you need. At the store or dealership, try to find out if the salespeople are working toward special incentives. In the absence of that information, ask the salesperson if he or she will be rewarded for selling a particular product to you. If you get an honest answer, you know how you might be able to influence the agent to lower the price.

Suggested Reading

Burger, Sanchez, Imberi, and Grande, "The Norm of Reciprocity as an Internalized Social Norm."

Carnegie, *Dale Carnegie's Lifetime Plan for Success.*

Pink, *To Sell Is Human.*

Activities to Try

1. In your next service encounter, learn your server's name and use it. Also, ask something personal about the server and use that information. Most importantly, smile. See if these efforts affect the type of service you receive. To test the effectiveness of this approach, ask for something special that requires extra effort and see if you get it.

2. The next time you're in the market to make a big purchase, give yourself plenty of time to do research about product features and costs. If you can, find out if your sales representative is working toward any incentives.

Selling and Being Sold
Lecture 9—Transcript

Think back to your best encounter with a salesperson, service, agent, or waiter. Close your eyes for a minute and return to that situation. If you're driving right now, let's keep the eyes open, but still, picture the events in your mind. What did that person say and do that made the experience so satisfying, so memorable? Recall some of the topics we've already covered in this course about likability as a characteristic of the agent, emotional appeal as a tactic. Perhaps the context was influential in some way too, with social proof. Now, think about the worst encounter you've ever had in these settings. This is a much less enjoyable exercise, but let's do it anyway. What happened? What did this person say or do that made the situation so irritating or frustrating? Again, it's likely that characteristics of the agent, narcissism or psychopathy, came into play along with characteristics of the context and perhaps even your own characteristic as a target of influence.

In this lecture, we're going to focus specifically on sales and service situations to apply some of what we've learned to those all-too-frequent events in our day-to-day life. What happens in these situations that makes them fantastic or terrible? As part of this lecture we'll also talk about ways that you can apply principles of influence to turn the tables on overly pushy sales agents. How can you get a better deal from your sales encounters by applying the concepts you're learning in this course?

I want to begin by telling you about my biggest shopping spree and the sales agent who made it happen. I will call her Joyce, just to make it easy, although that's not her real name, and I will call the store Great Guy Clothing. I'm not in the business of taking money for product endorsements. The first time I entered Great Guy Clothing, I was on a trip out of town, and I had never even heard of the store. I quickly found that I liked the clothing and appreciated the low key but professional approach to service. Joyce had approached me as I entered, introduced herself, and offered help. I initially declined and was left alone.

When I finally did decide to try on pants, she seemed to sense it and was there and ready to help. She took me to a dressing room. When I came out to look in the mirror, Joyce was there quietly waiting to see if she could be of further help. She only offered a comment when asked, and she complimented me but in a brief, genuine way. She made a suggestion that there were other styles and colors that I might like as well and offered to help by getting them. With her help, I tried on a few more. Her comments to me were straightforward, expert, and honest. As we talked, she asked a few questions and learned a bit about me. I decided to buy a pair of pants that day, and she made everything quite easy, tailoring was included, as was shipping back to my house in Iowa, so I didn't have to worry about returning to pick up the pants. It was a great experience, and in the months that followed, I appreciated the quality of the pants.

The real shopping spree happened when I returned eight months later, a testament, I think, to the idea that real influence happens through relationships that are built over time. On my return trip I walked into the door of the store, and she immediately greeted me with, "Welcome back, Professor Brown. Glad to see you made the trip from Iowa. How are you enjoying the pants? Were you looking for something specific today, perhaps a sports coat and shirt to match?" I left that day with three more pairs of pants, two shirts, two ties, and a sports coat. To this day, it was my biggest single-store shopping spree.

This type of service is not magic, as it is exactly what high-end merchants do every day. So let's analyze what Joyce did right. Let's talk about the characteristics of sales agents who are great at what they do, as well as the tactics they use to close the deal. We'll talk about tactics so you can appreciate good sales when you see it and so you can avoid getting suckered in when it's something you really don't need to buy.

In my own story, Joyce was fantastic, because she was both competent, she knew the clothes, and also caring, she took the time to get to know and remember me. If you recall from our conversation about agent characteristics and tactics, competent and caring are two fundamental characteristics of people that have a big influence on whether we trust them. Joyce's behavior is also consistent with some of the most practical work ever written on influence. We haven't talked about this so far, but now is a good time to bring in the classic work of none other than Dale Carnegie.

Carnegie is best remembered for his best-selling book *How to Win Friends and Influence People*. Carnegie was born in Missouri in 1888, grew up milking cows, and then worked in a series of sales jobs. After failing in an attempt to become an actor, he got the idea to teach public speaking and met with great success. Carnegie went on to teach and write, eventually publishing the international bestseller in 1936. The publisher, Simon and Schuster, estimates that that book has sold more than 15 million copies. The core idea behind Carnegie's work is that by changing your own behavior you can become more confident, better liked, and more persuasive. Among other pieces of advice, Carnegie offered six simple suggestions for how you can get people to like you. Let's review them briefly and note how Joyce did with regard to each.

First, Carnegie suggested, be genuinely interested in people. Joyce showed this by being attentive to me at every point without being overbearing and by asking questions to get to know me. Second, remember and use people's names. Dale Carnegie once said, "A person's name is to that person the sweetest sound and most important sound in any language." Joyce made use of this knowledge and remembered me. She used my name right away and again throughout all of our encounters. Third, be a good listener. When Joyce asked questions, she really listened and used that information, not just that day, but even eight months later.

Fourth on Carnegie's list, talk to people in terms of their own interests. Good sales people do this naturally. The conversation should be about the customer and his needs, not about the company or the salesperson. Joyce focused on me and my clothing needs. Fifth, make people feel important and do it sincerely. One of the best ways to do this, and again, Joyce succeeded here, is to remember someone's name and other facts about that person and use that information to create a genuine personal interaction. And sixth on the list is smile. It's simple, but powerful. In each of our encounters, Joyce had a smile on her face.

How does Carnegie's work hold up when studied by hospitality scholars in today's modern society? A paper by Michael Lynn, from Cornell's School of Hotel Administration, reviewed a large number of studies on what servers can do to increase their tips. He suggested that the largest increase in restaurant tipping was not for using the customer's name, but for something even simpler. Can you guess what it is? Let's review some of Lynn's estimates. Using the customer's name, 10 percent increase in tips; giving customer candy, 18 to 21 percent increase in tips; squatting down next to the table, 20 to 25 percent increase; mirroring by repeating orders back yielded 100 percent increase in tips. That's double, but there's still one effect that was even larger. Can you guess it? Smiling. The estimate is that servers who smile broadly and genuinely, compared to those who didn't, is a 140 percent increase in tips.

Because smiling works so well, let's talk about it further. What is it about a smile that opens people up to influence? Doug Pugh, in a research study published in the *Academy of Management Journal*, suggested two reasons that a positive event like a genuine smile can make people feel better about their encounter with a server or sales agent. First, there is a general expectation that people in those kinds of roles will be nice and helpful. A smile signifies kindness and builds confidence that you will be helped and get what you seek from that encounter. Second, the smile may operate via an emotional contagion to put the customer in a good mood.

And emotional contagion is exactly what it sounds like, the idea that moods can actually be caught, transmitted between people. I mentioned that in an earlier lecture about yawns, that they're catching. The same can be said for smiles. And, when you're put in a good mood, customers will be more likely to evaluate any exchange positively. That's actually the hallmark of good moods. Everything seems better when you're in a good mood, including the service, exchange, or product you just bought. A truly genuine smile can be thought of as creating a warm, positive feeling in you that then permeates how you see and judge everything that happens next.

Pugh's results support these ideas. He studied this with bank tellers and found that customers were in better moods and rated their exchange with the bank more positively when the person serving them smiled. Of course, not everyone reacts the same way with emotional contagion. If you are in a seriously deep mood state, it may be hard for an outside event to alter it. And it might not surprise you to know that people who register high on psychopath scales are less influenced by other people's mood states, and in fact, may display an opposite reaction. That is, such a person might actually smile in response to someone's negative emotional display. That's a disturbing idea, but it's certainly consistent with what we discussed in our lecture on the dark triad. So here again, we see that characteristics of the agent and target work together in determining the outcome of an attempt to influence.

So far we've been focused on characteristics of the agent, the person who's providing a service or trying to make a sale. Another part of our ATTiC model is characteristics of the target, that is, in these situations, the buyer. In previous lectures we noted that some people are more suggestible than others. Are some people more likely to buy following an encounter with a sales agent? Here there are two ideas I want to discuss, both of which are captured in common wisdom about how to shop. The first wise piece of advice is don't go to the grocery store hungry. The second is don't buy what you don't need. Let's talk about each.

Don't go to the grocery store hungry is a warning to not go shopping when you are likely to think everything looks great. And it's true, at least for me. I've been to the grocery store after a long day of work with no lunch, and I came home with so many bags of groceries that I had to fill the trunk and the back seat. My wife laughed when she saw me carrying these arm loads of groceries, and she knew exactly what had happened. The bigger idea here is that when you are strongly motivated to buy, your pursuit of that goal may lead you to be less rational in considering whether and what to buy. When your goal, for example, is to buy the car, your focus may be on that goal and only that goal; you may not consider other possibilities, such as walking away if the deal isn't good or waiting for another day when you can get a better deal. So, we should follow the advice of this piece of wisdom about grocery shopping, but we should also extend it to other situations. If you can, don't wait until your computer crashes or your car stops to shop for new ones. Start looking in advance, set a budget, and examine the features of products based on what you need.

The other piece of advice is don't buy what you don't need. This can be surprisingly difficult too. One summer I lived at the beach, living as a student, as students often do, eating primarily beans, rice, and noodles. After one particularly long night of work, I woke up early to go shopping. I went to get the essentials, cereal, toilet paper, and beans. My friends and I were sleepily standing in the isle talking when we heard someone calling people over for a product demonstration. We walked over, stood with the big crowd, and listened to what turned out to be a very persuasive agent. I let myself walk away that day with something I really didn't need living at the beach, a pen set. It went unused. Why did I buy? Certainly the sales person was good, but I also blame my own tiredness. I was too tired to resist.

To make sure you don't end up with too many groceries or a pen set you don't need, you should avoid sales situations when you are highly motivated to buy or when you are too tired to resist. If that situation can't be avoided, you can at least slow things down and fix in your mind that you will not buy now and walk away. Sales agents often try to make sure this does not happen, because they want you to act in the moment. But you should walk away and dispel the idea that you absolutely have to buy. Then, rather than consider why you should buy, consider the reasons why you should not buy. This may help to displace the commitment that is biasing your thoughts in support of a purchase.

We've talked about agent and target characteristics in sales situations. Let's continue discussing the ATTiC model by moving to context. There are certain contexts that create a strong push for sales agents to sell, sell, sell. For example, with the launch of my first textbook, the publishing company decided that they really wanted to get a foothold on the market, so they doubled sales commissions. That meant that sales reps would get double their usual commission for selling our book over any other book in their sales catalog. I was certainly grateful for that decision, as I actually witnessed the company's sales reps knocking on extra doors trying to get sales. With the strong incentive to sell, most sales reps will work harder to pursue leads and close deals.

In many sales industries, there are incentives, just like this, or even contests, such that someone who sells the most receives an award. Perhaps the most famous example of sales incentives comes from Mary Kay cosmetics. Representatives of this company who meet certain sales goals can get a car with no lease payment and only a nominal insurance payment. It used to only be pink Cadillacs, but the program has since expanded.

Reviewing sales contests I've found research indicates sales people are best motivated by contests where multiple people can win. For those of you who have done sales as a living, this is immediately obvious. How hard would you compete with 500 other people for one award? In contrast, if half of the sales agents can win, so long as they hit a particular sales level, then you see your chances as significantly better and will be more likely to work hard to get sales.

In this way, sales people are just like all of us. If they're going to work harder, they would like to see a reasonable chance that it will be rewarded. This is, in fact, the prediction of one of the best established economic theories of human motivation, expected utility theory. Psychologists often prefer the term expectancy theory, but many of the predictions are the same. People will work harder if they believe the extra effort is likely to yield a meaningful reward. Many companies recognize this and have a range of different awards available for their sales agents or when they hit different levels of sales.

What does this mean for you? The implication is clear. If you understand the ways in which your sale may help the sales person, then you may find yourself in a better bargaining position. Let's talk in more detail about one particular purchase that many of us don't enjoy, buying cars. An article on car buying published in MSN Money noted that many of the tips floating around about when and how to bargain for cars are myths. Specifically, you may have read that you should visit the dealer at the end of the week or end of month. But visiting at these times may not help if you think about how dealer incentives work. For one thing, there is variability in the incentives from dealers, and not all of them work on traditional weekly and monthly calendars. You may not know the actual start and end dates for incentives and competitions, and the sales person may already have met a magical threshold, so he may not really need your sale, and, if lots of people follow the advice of buying late in the week or month, then sales agents will be busier and feel they have greater leverage to walk away from a reasonable, let alone, a lowball offer.

If these aren't great pieces of advice, what is better advice? One of the best things you can do is to educate yourself about the incentives that may be in place. Edmunds.com and Kelley Blue Book often offer information about incentives from the dealer, and this will allow you to understand when incentives may end. Local dealers don't advertise those incentives, but you could certainly ask. Often the best way to find the best deal is simply a matter of economics. Where the demand is lowest, companies often put sales incentives in place to move inventory, so check for incentives on those low-demand cars, and seek a dealership that has many on the lot.

Another possibility is to seek out a dealership that does not pay commission on cars. We have just such a dealership north of me in Cedar Rapids, Iowa. The owner grew up selling cars and believes strongly in repeat business. So he puts his sales agents on salary. His sales agents are paid to be good to customers, not to close deals. And this dealership is not unique. In his book *To Sell is Human*, Daniel Pink suggests that the best sales professionals should be paid to provide great service, not just to sell. He offers other examples of companies, like Microchip Technologies, who have abandoned commissions, so the context of sales encounters is really about service and not about closing the deal.

We've just talked about how sales contests and pay structures create a context that can influence sales agents' behavior. Another important context feature is reciprocity. If someone has done you a favor recently, you will feel a natural obligation to return that favor. Just how powerful is this push within our minds to pay back? Jerry Burger, the professor who replicated the Milgram compliance studies, also studied the power of reciprocity. In a simple experiment involving 120 undergraduate students, participants came into a lab to do a simple set of tasks. The tasks weren't relevant to the study, as what was really studied was how participants would react when they were given an unexpected favor.

Here's how the experiment worked. Two students were sitting in a room. One of them was an actual participant. The other was a research confederate. After a few minutes, the research confederate would excuse herself to go to the restroom. Upon returning, she would say that she had been offered leftover bottles of water from a club meeting, and she picked up two, one for herself and one for the real research participant. There was also a condition where upon return, the confederate said nothing and just returned to her seat. We'll call this the no favor condition to contrast it with the favor condition, where a water bottle was given.

When the experiment was ostensibly over, the very same confederate would ask the participant to complete a survey that she created for a class. The survey was to be completed and returned to a different office in the same building, but three days later, so there was an element of inconvenience with the survey, even though it only contained 12 items. To be helpful to the research confederate, a participant would have to do the work and then remember to return it three days later. Who complied and completed the survey? With no favor, the rates were very low, further indicating the inconvenience of this little ask, averaging 5 percent. But when the favor had been given, the rates jumped to 28 percent. With a small favor, compliance was five times the amount.

There was another wrinkle to this study. Burger and his colleagues also tested whether it mattered to tell the participant that the confederate, this is the one who gave the water bottle, would be physically present when the survey was turned in. It didn't matter much at all, as compliance rates were slightly higher when the confederate wasn't even planning to be there, so this is not a matter of having developed a personal attachment. It's a generalized obligation that we feel to pay back someone when they've done something for us. Burger and his colleagues concluded that the desire to reciprocate a favor is so fundamental and ingrained that we want to do it even if no one knows that we are doing it.

Because this effect is so powerful, we see sales agents giving away little gifts all the time. At the dealer where they service my car, there are free water bottles, apples, and donuts. When books reps visit me to sell their textbooks, they sometimes bring along snacks. Drug reps are known for doing this as well, as much as the law will allow nowadays.

To counteract the influence of these gifts, some hospitals, big companies, and governments have specific policies that limit the amount and type of gift that can be given. As a branch of the Iowa state government, faculty, staff, and administrators at the University of Iowa, where I work, are limited to gifts valued at $5 or less. A student in my class can buy me a regular cup of coffee, if they were hoping to influence me, but not a venti vanilla bean Frappuccino from Starbucks. I think they're costing now $25?

I say this all in jest because knowing what I know about reciprocity, I don't let students buy me things or give me gifts. I know that even if I try hard not to be influenced, the natural psychological processes that result from reciprocity will be operating in my mind. Amway, one of the largest and best-known direct sales operations, larger even than Mary Kay cosmetics, teaches sales agents to use this technique by encouraging them to host parties where you serve snacks and beverages and give away small sample packets. After eating a cheese cube, drinking a glass of wine, being handed a small sample, it's hard to do anything other than reciprocate and buy something.

Counteracting reciprocity is hard because it is a natural psychological process, but there are things you can do. For example, thinking about the Amway or Mary Kay party, you might abstain from eating or accepting a gift, or if this is someone you really like you might bring a small gift to the host. Either way, you should feel less compelled to buy, unless it's something you really want.

For the agents, targets, and context effects that I have presented I offered a few suggestions. Knowing what we know about how the human mind works, it will help you if you understand the subtle influences that an agent's smile, your own desire to buy, and a little gift can have on your willingness to buy. How can you use this knowledge? Here are two things you can try. First, in your next service encounter, learn your server's name, use it, and ask something personal about that person and use that information. Most importantly, smile. See if that changes the type of service you receive. If you really want to test the effectiveness this produces on your service provider, ask for something special that requires extra effort. See if you get it.

Second, the next time you go for a big purchase, make sure to give yourself time. Don't wait until the last minute, and do an online search about information that will tell you features and costs. This will help you avoid getting caught up and buying something that meets your immediate goal to buy, but doesn't give you what you need. See if there are any incentives that the sales folks are under. In the absence of that information you might try a direct approach. Ask your sales rep if she would be rewarded for selling any particular product to you. You might just get an honest answer and then you know where you might be able to influence her to lower the price.

Just as this lecture helps us apply lessons of influence to sales situations, these tips help us apply research findings about sales agents, contexts, and tactics to our advantage. We'll turn next to the topic that makes a lot of people more nervous than buying a car, making speeches. If you'd like to be less nervous and more persuasive the next time you talk in front of a group, then join me for the next lecture.

Delivering Effective Speeches
Lecture 10

Robert Kennedy's announcement of the assassination of Martin Luther King on April 4, 1968, is considered to be among the most moving speeches in U.S. history. What made this speech influential, and more broadly, what are the components of an effective speech? In this lecture, we will address these questions by drawing on the insights of both the ancient and the modern world. First, we'll go to the man who is generally considered to be the founder of rhetoric in the West, Aristotle. Then, we will discuss how Aristotle's ideas were elaborated on by the Roman orator Cicero. Finally, we'll end closer in time to the present by reviewing Dale Carnegie's tips for effective speaking.

Ethos
- Aristotle described three tools or techniques available to a speaker trying to persuade an audience: ethos, logos, and pathos. Ethos refers to the audience's perception of a speaker's character. A speaker who generates perceptions of credibility and trust will be more effective in convincing an audience.
    o Note here the focus on the agent characteristics we talked about earlier in this course. Aristotle argued that the agent's character matters and that a speaker can say specific things to convince the audience that he or she is worth listening to.

    o Aristotle suggested that ethos requires a perception of intelligence and good will on the part of the audience, two characteristics that overlap with the qualities of competence and caring that we have discussed.

- Aristotle described a person of intelligence as one who is sensible and sufficiently knowledgeable to address the topic at hand.

- The good will component of ethos requires the audience to perceive that the speaker is motivated not by self-interest, but by a genuine concern for the well-being of others.
  - One tactic for cultivating this perception is to seem reluctant about the issue of concern. For example, you might say that you didn't believe something until you were confronted with overwhelming evidence. In his documentary *An Inconvenient Truth*, Al Gore used this technique to describe the effect that overwhelming evidence of carbon dioxide emissions had on his views about global warming.

  - At times, this approach to creating an impression of good will can be disingenuous and may cross an ethical line. If you feign surprise about information that changed your mind (when the audience knows that your mind was already made up), then you could undermine your credibility and any chance you have of being influential in the future.

Logos
- Logos relates to the argument itself and how it should be shaped to be most convincing. At the heart of every speech is a core argument—a claim with associated evidence that you are making to compel people to believe or act in a certain way.

- Aristotle noted—and it's is still true today—that many arguments are not well constructed and contain logical fallacies.
  - One fallacy that Aristotle pointed out is equivocation, which occurs when a speaker is not clear about his or her intended meaning. In equivocating, a speaker may be trying to "get away with" a weak argument. But this strategy can undermine the speaker's effectiveness, particularly if the audience is listening carefully.

  - Another fallacy is the ad hominem argument, that is, an argument based on a characteristic of a person rather than on sound evidence and logic. We often see this fallacy in action when politicians attempt to disparage their opponents.

Although such attacks are not logical, they sometimes work, particularly if they are connected to valid issues. Ad hominem attacks also take advantage of social proof; if enough people believe that a politician's opponent is a fool or liar, then the idea will take on the color of truth, with the result that the opponent will lose at least some capacity to influence others.

- Even though fallacies are often used successfully in political debates, they are best considered a crutch when good arguments are in short supply. What politicians and other speakers should do is focus on building logos with clear and logically consistent claims.

Pathos

- Pathos refers to the emotions experienced by the audience during a speech. Aristotle's idea here was that speakers should elicit emotions that are germane to the argument being made. The goal is to inspire certain emotions in your listeners so that they will be more likely to understand your perspective, accept your claims, and act on your suggestions.

- Speakers can inspire pathos quite effectively using vivid language and a story, which may help connect abstract arguments with concrete images.

- The type of emotion that should be elicited, and how intense it is, depends on the nature of the speaker's goals. Sometimes a mild emotion, such as slight nervousness about the future, is sufficient. If the speaker is trying to move people to action, then a more intense emotion may be needed.

Robert Kennedy on Martin Luther King

- In his speech announcing the death of Martin Luther King, Robert Kennedy's logos was clear and impeccable. He said that King had lived and died for peace and would have wanted to see his vision of a united America come to pass rather than experience more violence.

- Kennedy also effectively employed pathos. The emotions of grief and loss came through in his voice, and he did not try to hide them. The members of his audience were in shock—confused, sad, and angry. Kennedy did not shy away from acknowledging these emotions; in fact, he even showed his own sadness. In this way, Kennedy made a strong connection with the audience.

President Ronald Reagan has been labeled the "great communicator," and his speeches offer wonderful examples of the use of pathos.

© U.S. Department of Defense/Wikimedia Commons/public domain.

- Finally and perhaps most importantly, Kennedy referenced his personal experience to generate ethos. He presented himself as a man who had also lost someone dear to him. He had intelligence drawn from personal experience, and he showed good will toward the crowd by not attempting to hide difficult news and by acknowledging the very real tension between blacks and whites.

The Roman Orator Cicero

- Cicero joined the Roman Senate in 75 B.C. and argued there for many years. He introduced the five canons of persuasion: invention, arrangement, style, memory, and delivery.
  - o Under the heading of invention, Cicero argued that a speaker must prepare a speech by seeking out specific information and tools needed to persuade the audience on the specific topic of concern. For our purposes, that means that you should do your research and think about the most compelling reasons for the audience to believe that your ideas are good ones.

- Arrangement refers to putting together the structure of an argument. Think about the flow of your argument, typically beginning with ethos to win the crowd over, proceeding to logos to establish the argument, and finally, sealing the deal with pathos.

- Style should be carefully considered to produce the desired emotional reaction in the audience. According to Cicero, a speaker should think about which emotion best serves an argument and use a style that elicits it. Thumping the podium and shouting may be great for pumping up a group of marchers, but it won't work in most business conferences. Match the style of your speech to the event and your goals as a speaker.

- Memory simply means speaking without having to refer to notes. You should know who you are talking about and focus your entire attention on the audience, not on your PowerPoint slides.

- Finally, delivery refers to practicing to make sure that you are acting out your speech in a way that best conveys the message.

- Although some of Cicero's canons now seem dated, such as memorizing and acting out a speech, they can be quite impressive if used properly. Consider the impression of intelligence and competence created by giving a speech from memory and matching your gestures and body language to your words.

- In his book *Thank You for Arguing*, Jay Heinrichs provides a helpful summary of Cicero's tips. Heinrichs suggests using language that the audience understands, being clear, being vivid, following local conventions, and having a little ornament but not too much.

- Together, Aristotle and Cicero provide a good overview of classical views of argument and influence. Although these ideas predate the theory and research we've discussed thus far in the course by about 2,000 years, they have stood the test of time. Despite the monumental changes in how we communicate, the suggestions of Aristotle and Cicero still are useful.

Dale Carnegie
- In the last lecture, we talked about Carnegie's six tips for getting people to like you. In his classic book, Carnegie also offers three fundamental principles for handling people that can be adapted to speech making. His short list is as follows:
  - o Don't criticize, condemn, or complain.

  - o Give honest and sincere appreciation.

  - o Arouse in your audience an "eager want."

- In giving a speech, these three principles complement and add to the ideas of Aristotle and Cicero. They reinforce the concern for ethos by asking the speaker to focus on positives, showing evidence of good will. The act of giving honest appreciation, such as acknowledging listeners for their good work, also allows the audience to recognize the speaker's intelligence.

- Arousing an "eager want" means connecting with people and spurring them to action. For Carnegie, the key here is to choose as your topic something about which you are genuinely passionate. It's nearly impossible to get others to feel passion if you don't feel it yourself, and trying to act it out is best left to the professionals. Instead, you should craft a speech that allows you to discuss what you know and care deeply about. If you do that, the audience will want to listen and will be more likely to be persuaded.

Application: Speaking Effectively
- Watch a political speech and look for signs of ethos, logos, and pathos. A good speech will show signs of each. If the speech falls flat, think about what was missing. Did the speaker forget to connect and establish credibility with the audience via ethos? Were the arguments hard to follow—a sign of poorly developed logos?

Perhaps the emotional tone of the speaker did not match the speech or the desired action. If so, then the failure is with pathos.

- Draft your own speech. Consider a topic of importance to you and identify a time and place when you will be given the floor to speak your mind. To follow the tips here, you need to decide on a goal (what you want your audience to do) and identify what the audience already knows and feels. With that information, you can invent and arrange the argument. Then, take the time to practice your speech and get some feedback.

Suggested Reading

Carnegie, *How to Win Friends and Influence People.*

Heinrichs, *Thank You for Arguing.*

Activities to Try

1. Watch a political speech. Look for the signs of ethos, logos, and pathos. A good speech will show signs of each. If the speech falls flat, what was missing?

2. Draft your own speech. Identify a topic of importance to you and imagine a time and place when you will be given the floor to speak your mind. You should have a clear goal in mind, and you should be cognizant of what the audience already knows and feels. With that information, you can invent and arrange your argument. Next, practice your speech and get some feedback.

Real-World Influence Scenario

Imagine that you want to persuade the members of your local church congregation to pitch in to help with a major community project. How can you craft a speech that moves the congregation to action?

To address Aristotle's ethos, you need to inspire in your audience the perception of intelligence. You can do this by mentioning your relevant experience in the congregation and specific accomplishments of church volunteer efforts you've assisted with in the past. You can also speak about how proud you are to have been part of those past efforts. Without bragging about what you can do as a leader, you are convincing the audience that you know what you're talking about when it comes to church volunteer efforts and that you've been an integral part of previous successes.

Now imagine that you have won over your local congregation and are giving your speech in another place, perhaps a church in a Southern city. In that case, sprinkling additional polite terms into your speech and slowing down the pace of your words would allow you to fit in better and make you more likely to be persuasive. You might also refer to the culture and traditions of the city to show the audience members that you understand and appreciate their background.

Delivering Effective Speeches
Lecture 10—Transcript

Robert Kennedy was on the campaign trail in April 1968 and was heading for an event in Indianapolis where he'd be speaking to a largely black crowd in a poor neighborhood. On the way, he learned that the reverend Martin Luther King Jr. had been assassinated in Memphis. He was also told that few, if any, of the people in the crowd would have heard the tragic news. The local police feared that violence would erupt once word of the assassination spread, and they told Kennedy that they could not protect him if that happened, so it would have been perfectly reasonable for Kennedy just to bypass the event, but is that what he did?

Kennedy, instead, stood on the back of a flatbed truck, faced the crowd, and broke the news of King's assassination right away. He spoke for less than five minutes that day and gave what some considered to be among the best speeches in U.S. history. He said,

> "I have some very sad news for all of you, and, I think, sad news for all of our fellow citizens, and people who love peace all over the world; and that is that Martin Luther King was shot and killed tonight in Memphis, Tennessee."

In recordings of the speech, gasps can be heard in the audience along with an outcry of surprise and sadness. Kennedy spoke on to memorialize King by explaining that King had dedicated his life to love and justice. Kennedy then asked the crowd, what direction do we want to take as a country, toward hate and anger, or toward the goal that Martin Luther King worked and died for, toward compassion and love? Then Kennedy did something quite unusual. Prior to this moment he had rarely spoken publicly about his brother's assassination, but, in addressing that largely African-American crowd in Indianapolis that day, he made very clear reference to it. He spoke to the people who might feel hate and anger and said,

> "For those of you who are black and are tempted to be filled with hatred and mistrust of the injustice of such an act against all white people, I would only say that I can also feel in my own heart this

same kind of feeling. I had a member of my family killed and he was killed by a white man."

Kennedy went on to call for unity regardless of race and called for people to say a prayer for MLK's family and for our country, a prayer for understanding and compassion. The crowd applauded and dispersed quietly without violence. Meanwhile, in more than 100 cities across the United States, riots erupted.

What makes this an influential speech? And more broadly, what are the components of an effective speech, whether given at a political rally, a community fund-raising event, a presentation at work, or even a dinner party? Imagine you decide to stand up for a cause that matters to you and give a speech at your local church. How could you craft something that moves the crowd toward a desired action?

In this lecture, we're going to address these questions by drawing on the insights of both the ancient and the modern world. First, we'll go to the man who is generally considered to be the founder of rhetoric in the West—Aristotle. Then we'll discuss how Aristotle's ideas were elaborated on by the Roman orator, Cicero. Finally, we'll end closer to our current time by reviewing Dale Carnegie's tips for effective speaking.

Let's start with Aristotle, who believed that there were three tools, or techniques, available to a speaker trying to persuade her audience, ethos, logos, and pathos. The first technique a speaker uses is ethos. Ethos refers to the audience's perception of a speaker's character. A speaker who generates perceptions of credibility and trust will be better able to convince the audience. This is, in fact, a focus on those agent characteristics that we talked about earlier in this course when I introduced the ATTiC model. Aristotle was arguing that the agent's characteristics matter, and that there are quite specific things that a speaker can say to convince the audience, I am worth listening to.

If you recall from the lecture about impression management, research has shown that there are two characteristics that people naturally and quite quickly assess about others, competence and caring. The overlap with

Aristotle here is fascinating, as he suggests that ethos requires, as part of a short list, a perception of intelligence and of goodwill to the audience. If we take intelligence for competence and goodwill for caring, there's quite a bit of consistency between the ideas from the ancient world and the modern world of empirical research.

What did Aristotle mean by intelligence, and how did he suggest that you could make sure an audience sees you that way? Someone with intelligence, as Aristotle describes it, is a sensible person, one who holds common sense and is sufficiently knowledgeable to address the topic at hand. So let's say you're in a situation where you want to persuade your local church congregation to pitch in to help with a major community project. How can you stand up and propose this idea in such a way that your intelligence shines through? Well, it can be useful to mention your relevant experience in the congregation. Mention the specific accomplishments that you've witnessed in the past when the church came together, and you, with them, volunteered and made great things happen. Go on to talk about how proud you've been to be part of those efforts. Without bragging about what you can do as a leader, you are convincing the audience that you know what you're talking about when it comes to church volunteer efforts, and that you've been an integral part of past success.

Aristotle also discussed goodwill as a component of ethos. If you want to deliver a successful speech, then the audience needs to perceive that you are motivated, not by self-interest, but by a genuine concern for the well-being of the audience. How do you cultivate that perception? To convey goodwill, you might seem to be reluctant about something you're trying to convince your audience about. Note, for example, that you didn't believe something, just as the audience might not now, until you were confronted with overwhelming evidence. In his documentary *An Inconvenient Truth*, Al Gore used this technique to describe the effect that overwhelming evidence of CO_2 emissions had on his views about global warming. Whether you agree with his conclusions or not, if you watch the movie you can see how effective perceptions of good will are in drawing listeners into the argument.

On the other hand, I worry some that this approach to creating an impression of goodwill might be seen as disingenuous and may cross an ethical line.

If you feign surprise about information that changed your mind, when the audience really knows your mind was already made up, then you could undermine your credibility and any chance of being influential going into the future. Nonfictional speeches are not fictional theatre or made up. While we can learn from theatre, we have to be careful about making things up, going too far and adopting techniques that could be perceived as manipulative.

So far we've been talking about Aristotle's first means of persuasion, ethos. To sum up, we can say that ethos is a means of persuasion, a technique that bolsters the speaker's perceived character. By conveying intelligence and goodwill, speakers are more likely to succeed in their attempt to influence. Now, let's discuss Aristotle's second technique for persuasion, logos. Logos relates to the argument itself and how it should be shaped to be most convincing. At the heart of every speech is a core argument, a claim with associated evidence that you're making to compel people to believe or act in a certain way. Aristotle noted, and this is still true today, that many arguments are not well constructed and contain logical fallacies. Fallacies are flaws in arguments that we should avoid if we wish to be influential speakers, so let's spend a few moments looking at a couple of common fallacies that speakers commit.

One fallacy that Aristotle pointed out is equivocation. This is when someone uses a word that has multiple meanings and is not clear about the intended meaning. For example, when an employee who is often late to work is asked by her supervisor, "When did you get to work?" she might respond "some time ago." In her mind, she knows that some time ago refers to 15 minutes, but she's hoping that her boss will interpret this to mean much earlier. Or take an example of delivering a speech to a church congregation. The speaker might claim that he met the President of the United States, who supports this work. Here, "met" might literally mean that he shook hands briefly with the president, and "this work" may refer to any type of community development. But by using vague words, the speaker implies a more personal connection took place, and that the President endorses this particular church project.

In the case of the short conversation with the boss and the church speech, a speaker who uses equivocation may be trying to get away with a weak argument, but this is a dubious strategy that can undermine your effectiveness, particularly if an audience is listening carefully. Instead of using equivocation, it would be far better for you to carefully attend to logos. This involves thinking through the pieces of evidence that should convince the audience, then laying that argument out with a thoughtful selection of words and phrases. If you go this route, Aristotle would be pleased.

Another fallacy is the ad hominem argument. This is when we base an argument on a characteristic of a person, rather than on sound evidence and logic. We often see this fallacy in action with ad hominem attacks, in which speakers disparage the character of another person in an attempt to discredit his argument. In a famous example that shows U.S. politics has always been a rough sport, the campaign between John Adams and Thomas Jefferson in 1800 was hotly contested; it was actually a rematch of the 1796 election that Adams had won. During the campaign, supporters of Adams called Jefferson an "uncivilized atheist" and a "tool for the godless French." He was also called a weakling and the "son of a half-breed Indian squaw." Supporters of Jefferson called Adams a "fool, a gross hypocrite and an unprincipled oppressor" who had a "hermaphroditical character ... with neither the force and firmness of a man nor the gentleness and sensibility of a woman." There were other attacks in U.S. political history, further proof that negative campaigning is not a modern invention. For example, in the contest between John Quincy Adams and Andrew Jackson in 1828, Quincy Adams was called a pimp, and Jackson's wife was dragged in the mud with some pretty mean labels as well.

Considering how clearly vicious some of these attacks are, why do people use them? The answer is simple. Ad hominem attacks can work, even if they're not always logical. To begin, we should note that sometimes the attacks have some connection to valid political issues. For example, to call John Adams an oppressor could be relevant to his views about the appropriate range of central government authority. And to discuss Jefferson's connection to the French could be relevant to his likely foreign policy. To the extent that these issues are important to the campaign and the choice of how one might vote, then they are an important consideration.

The problem with regard to logos arises when the labels are extended and exaggerated and then moved towards issues unrelated to the argument at hand, such as when Adams was called a fool and Jefferson a tool. These attacks are a blatant effort to rob the victim of ethos, and they can work if the audience does not take a critical approach to dissecting the argument to understand whether the claim is related at all to the argument at hand. As we've discussed in an earlier lecture, we can all be susceptible to social proof. If enough people can be enlisted to call your opponent a fool, a pimp, or a liar, then for some people, it will become truth, and the result is that your opponent will lose, at least, some capacity to influence others.

But even if fallacies are often used successfully in political debates, they are best considered a crutch when good arguments are in short supply. What these politicians should do, and I hope you will do as well, is focus on building logos with clear and logically consistent claims. If you have to resort to equivocation or ad hominem attacks, then maybe your position isn't that strong, and you should reconsider it.

Now that we've looked at ethos and logos, let's turn to the third and final technique addressed by Aristotle, pathos. Pathos refers to the emotions experienced by the audience during a speech. Aristotle was not endorsing arousing emotion in the audience just for the sake of doing so. His idea was that speakers should elicit emotions that are germane to the argument being made. The speaker's goal is to have an emotion present in the audience so that they will be more likely to understand your perspective, accept your claims, and act on your suggestions. This is often done quite effectively with the use of vivid language and a story, which helps put concrete images to the more abstract arguments being made. The type of emotion that should be elicited and how intense it is depends on the nature of the speaker's goals. Sometimes a mild emotion, a slight nervousness about the future, for example, is sufficient. If the speaker is trying to move people to action, then a more intense emotion might be needed.

President Ronald Reagan has been labeled the great communicator, and his speeches offer wonderful examples of pathos. Here's just one example drawn from his fifth State of the Union Address to the U.S. Congress in 1986.

"The American Dream is a song of hope that rings through night winter air. Vivid, tender music that warms our hearts when the least among us aspire to the greatest things; to venture a daring enterprise; to unearth new beauty in music, literature and art; to discover a new universe inside a tiny silicon chip or a single human cell."

Clearly, Reagan is tapping into the power of pathos by using vivid emotional language. Did he stop there? Of course not. To make this speech even more powerful, Reagan went on to tell the stories of specific young people who'd acted bravely to save their friends, who had created music, and served the poor. As if concrete and vivid stories were not enough, Reagan had these people actually attend the speech and stand up to be recognized when he finished. While they were standing, so the audience could see their faces, Reagan would continue:

"Thank you, thank you. You are heroes of our hearts. We look at you and know it's true: in this land of dreams fulfilled, where greater dreams may be imagined, nothing is impossible, no victory is beyond our reach, no glory will ever be too great."

Given the vividness of the language and the concreteness, even the presence of the specific people that he acknowledged, it's easy to see why Reagan was known as the great communicator. And if you've seen any State of the Union Address since 1986, this approach has become the norm. In starting this tradition of effective use of pathos, Reagan would have made Aristotle proud.

Now that we've covered ethos, logos, and pathos, let's revisit Robert Kennedy's short speech in 1968. Kennedy's logos was clear and impeccable. He was, in fact, saying what many other leaders were saying around the country, that Martin Luther King lived and died for peace, and he would have wanted to see his vision of a united America come to pass, rather than have more violence. The way to carry on King's legacy would not be through bloodshed, but through peace and unity.

Kennedy affectively employed pathos too. In his voice you could tell he felt loss and grief, and he didn't hide it. The members of the audience that day were in shock. They were confused, sad, and some, angry. Kennedy did not shy away from acknowledging these emotions. In fact, he even showed his own sadness. In this way, Kennedy connected with the audiences' emotions. Finally, and perhaps most importantly, Kennedy referenced his personal experience to generate ethos. This was a man who had also lost someone dear to him. He had intelligence drawn from personal experience, and he'd shown goodwill toward the crowd by facing and not shying away from difficult news, and by acknowledging very real tension between blacks and whites. One thing that really sticks with me about this speech, from the very first time I heard it, is that no one else could have given that speech, that night, the way Kennedy did. Who he was as a person blended with what he felt and believed to create a powerfully moving experience for the listeners. To use Aristotle's terms, it was in the careful adoption of ethos, logos, and pathos that a brilliant speech was crafted.

To continue our exploration of what makes for a great speech, let's move from the ancient Greeks forward in time, some, to ancient Rome, and the work of someone who's been called the best orator of all times, Cicero. Cicero joined the Roman Senate in 75 B.C. and argued there for many, many years. Let's review one of the most critical ideas that he offered, the five canons of persuasion: invention, arrangement, style, memory, and delivery.

Invention, Cicero argued, you must prepare your speech by seeking out specific information and tools you need to persuade your audience on the specific topic of the day. You should do your research and think about the most compelling reasons for the audience to believe that your ideas are the best ones.

Arrangement, this is putting together the structure of the argument. You should think about the flow of your argument, typically beginning with ethos to win the crowd over; proceeding to logos to establish the argument; and finally sealing the deal with pathos.

Next is style, which you should carefully consider in order to produce the desired emotional reaction in your audience. According to Cicero you should think about which emotion best serves your argument and use a style to elicit it. The podium-thumping, near-yelling staccato speech is great for pumping up an audience, but it won't work in most business conferences and certainly won't win any friends at a funeral. You should match the style to the event and your goals as a speaker.

Then comes memory, speaking without having to refer to notes. You should know what you are talking about and focus your entire attention on the audience, not on notes, or today's big mistake, PowerPoint slides, that might be showing behind you.

And finally, there is delivery. This is where you practice to make sure that you are acting out your speech in a way that best conveys the message.

Aristotle had discussed issues of style and delivery, but Cicero advanced these ideas by offering very detailed suggestions that are still taught in rhetoric classes today. While some now might seem dated, like memorizing and acting out a speech, they can be quite impressive if used properly. Consider the impression of intelligence and competence created by actually giving a speech from memory and matching all of your gestures and body language to the words spoken.

In his book, *Thank you for Arguing*, Jay Heinrichs provides a helpful summary of Cicero's tips. Heinrichs suggests using language that the audience understands, being clear, being vivid, following local conventions, and having a little ornament, but not too much. This means that you should adapt your words to the audience, and while not abandoning your own style or accent, you should find ways to connect with the people you're talking to.

Remember our example of convincing your local congregation to support a community project. Imagine that you win over your local congregation and are now giving a speech in another place. Imagine you moved from a northern church to the southern United States. In such a case, sprinkling additional polite terms into your speech and slowing down the pace of your words might allow you to fit in better and would make you likely more persuasive. Of course, you can take this too far. If you travel from your hometown in Boston to give a talk in Oxford, Mississippi, home of Ole Miss, you probably should not try to use phrases like y'all and down yonder. This would take you from trying to fit in to acting like an idiot by being inauthentic. Despite your best intentions, it might even be seen as patronizing.

What could you do in this circumstance? Well, to honor the culture and traditions of Ole Miss without pretending you are part of it, you should not mimic the language, but you could mention some things related to what locals care about. You might mention how excited you are to walk through the magnolia and oak trees in The Grove. The Grove is a beautiful tree-lined area that is central to campus, both physically and spiritually, as it's considered by some to be the greatest tailgating spot in all of college football.

Together, Aristotle and Cicero, provide a good overview of the classic views of argument and influence. While these ideas predate the theory and research we've discussed thus far by 2,000 years, it's amazing to me how well they've stood the test of time. Despite the monumental changes in how we communicate, the suggestions of Aristotle and Cicero are still useful. But what do more modern speech makers offer as advice for how to give an influential speech? Let's briefly return to Dale Carnegie, author of the classic bestseller, *How to Win Friends and Influence People*. We have talked about Carnegie's six tips for getting people to like you in the last lecture. In his book, Carnegie also offers three fundamental principles for handling people. And these principles can be adapted to speech making. His short list is, first, don't criticize, condemn, or complain; second, give honest and sincere appreciation; third, arouse in the other person an eager want.

In giving a speech, these three principles complement and add to the ideas of Aristotle and Cicero. To start, they reinforce the concern for ethos by asking you to focus on positives, showing goodwill. And of course, if you are giving honest appreciation, acknowledging your audience for their good work, then they will recognize your intelligence, as well as your good will. How do we arouse an eager want, which means connecting with people and spurring them to action? This is where Carnegie reinforces, and perhaps even adds to, the ideas from the ancient world. The key here is to talk about something that you have genuine passion about. I'm assuming here that you have some choice in topic, but even if you don't, you should try to connect your topic with things that matter to you. Why? Well, it's nearly impossible to get others to feel passion if you don't feel it yourself. And trying to act out being passionate is best left to the professionals. So instead of acting, you should craft a speech that you can talk about because you know and you care about the topic. And if you do that, the audience will want to listen, and they'll be more likely to be persuaded.

In this lecture, we have discussed Aristotle, Cicero, and now Carnegie, and along the way given you quite a few suggestions for preparing and delivering an influential speech. The speeches that you give do not have to be national addresses to benefit from these ideas. Pep talks you give your family, presentations at work, short speeches to local charity clubs, they can all be strengthened by applying the advice passed down from the ancient Greeks and Romans.

With that in mind, let me suggest two things to try from this lecture. First, watch a political speech. Look for the signs of ethos, logos, and pathos. A good speech will show signs of each. If the speech falls flat, think about what was missing. Did the speaker forget to connect and establish credibility with the audience via ethos? Or were the arguments hard to follow, a sign of poorly developed logos? Finally, perhaps the emotional tone of the speaker didn't match his speech or the desired action. If so, that's a failure in pathos.

Second, try drafting your own speech. Consider a topic of importance to you. Identify a time and place where you will be given the floor to speak your mind. Then, follow the tips here. You need to know what your goal is, what you want people to do, and what the audience already knows and feels. With that information you can invent and arrange the argument. Then, take the time to practice, get some feedback, commit it to memory. And then, how did you do with that delivery? Remember, practice and feedback. You'll get better.

In the next lecture, we will leave speeches and head for the negotiating table. We'll discuss things that you can do to be convincing when you're sitting across the table from someone, looking in their eyes, and trying to figure out the best way to close a deal.

Developing Negotiation Skills
Lecture 11

Herb Cohen, the author of the bestselling book *You Can Negotiate Anything*, calls the world a "giant negotiating table," and this characterization is correct. Negotiations happen around us all the time. Getting what you deserve out of a negotiation and having all parties walk away satisfied is a specific application of influence. Like all influence situations, negotiating well is a combination of art and science that can have profound implications for you; your coworkers, friends, and family members; and even society. In this lecture, we'll talk about how you can use influence successfully in negotiation settings—to reach an outcome that is considered fair by all parties.

Negotiation Scenario

"You are Dr. Jones, a biological research scientist employed by a pharmaceutical company. You have recently developed a synthetic chemical useful for curing a disease contracted by pregnant women. If not dealt with in the first four weeks of pregnancy, the disease causes serious brain, eye, and ear damage to the unborn child. Unfortunately, the serum is made from a rare fruit. Only about 4,000 were grown in the world this season.

"You have recently been told that a Mr. Cardoza, a South American fruit exporter, has 3,000 of these fruit. If you could obtain all 3,000, you could make enough serum from the juice to both cure all the present victims and inoculate all remaining pregnant women."

You have a budget of $250,000, but you aren't the only one seeking the fruit. Dr. Roland, who is employed by a competing pharmaceutical company, also hopes to get the fruit from Mr. Cardoza. Dr. Roland has been working on biological warfare research for the past several

Position-Based Negotiation

- Influence and negotiation have much in common, but there is an important difference between negotiation settings and the many examples of influence we've seen in this course. In a negotiation, people generally come together with the purpose of reaching an agreement; thus, negotiation is a concentrated time and space within which a variety of influence tactics may be applied. Because the parties are acutely aware that they are being subjected to influence, they are often guarded.

- In their book *Getting to Yes*, Roger Fisher and William Ury identify two broad negotiation strategies: principle-based negotiation and position-based negotiation. Fisher and Ury also describe three criteria that we should use to determine whether a negotiation tactic is successful: (1) It results in a settlement that is agreeable to both parties, (2) it is efficient, and (3) the parties are willing to work together again. When these three criteria are met, the negotiation is considered a win-win.

- Position-based negotiation occurs when each party focuses on a concrete position that must be obtained.
  - In the case of the rare fruit and your role as Dr. Jones, you might make Dr. Roland an offer, asking her to not seek the fruit in exchange for $100,000. That's effectively a cost of $100,000 for all 4,000 fruit produced worldwide.

  - You make this offer knowing that you actually have $250,000 to spend and need only 3,000 fruit. You've left yourself room to be "talked down" or "influenced" into paying a bit more or buying a bit less. But in the end, you know that you won't settle for any position that costs more than $250,000 and results in fewer than 3,000 fruit in hand. You are focused on the numbers.

- In the real world, a similar approach might be refusing to pay any more than $10,000 for a used car. In the case of home buying, a seller might refuse to pay any settlement costs, focusing the negotiation on making sure that all cash costs of the sale are covered by the buyer.

- In each case, a fixed monetary position is established that leads one party to see any outcome of the negotiation as either a win or a loss. Thus, position-based negotiation has also been called a win-lose approach. Adopting this approach sometimes inadvertently cuts off potentially creative solutions, and one person almost always walks away frustrated.

- The influence tactics used in position-based negotiation can vary, but they easily fall into hard tactics, such as pressure. When you get stuck on a particular number or single issue, then you may find yourself frustrated that the other party won't just "give in," and your frustration comes out in loudly stated demands or ultimatums.

Principle-Based Negotiation

- Principle-based negotiation involves exploring each party's underlying interests and seeking solutions that are mutually beneficial. Rather than pressure, a focus on interests pushes people toward the soft influence tactics of rational argument, inspiration, and exchange.

- In the real world, principle-based negotiations occur frequently. The exchange of power between two providers of electricity on the West Coast, with resulting environmental benefits, serves as a classic example.

- Research by Brandon Sullivan, Kathleen O'Connor, and Ethan Burris indicates that one of the most important agent characteristics

Conflict and lack of trust may play out in divorce proceedings; couples saddled with these issues are usually unwilling to propose win-win solutions.

leading to principle-based negotiation is confidence. Those who are confident that they can establish rapport, find trade-offs, and exchange concessions tend to be more likely to begin negotiations with the principle-based, win-win approach.

- The ATTiC model also reminds us that context matters. In the case of negotiations, a turbulent history that creates animosity and reduces trust makes it unlikely that creative solutions will emerge.

Position-Based Negotiation and the ATTiC Model

- In the area of context, research suggests that time pressure can contribute to the use of position-based negotiation. Under pressure, it is more difficult to take the time to exchange information, consider alternatives, and find a mutually beneficial solution. Technology may also play an important contextual role, leading to position-based negotiation. In a study conducted at Tel Aviv University, researchers found that people negotiating via e-mail used fewer soft and more hard tactics than those working face to face.

- With regard to the agent, a personal characteristic that may lead to a preference for position-based negotiation is competitiveness. In the United States, we often point to lawyers as the quintessential example here. Legal education in this country often socializes law students to be competitive to the point of aggressiveness. The result is a tendency for lawyers to adopt a position-based rather than a principle-based style.

- Another agent characteristic that might lead to choosing a position-based negotiation strategy is culture. As we discussed earlier, those from an individualist culture place their own goals and interests above the interests of the group. Those from a collectivist culture place the goals and interests of the group above their personal interests. Given these definitions, it might seem obvious that individualists would be more prone to position-based negotiation, but reality is a bit more complicated than that.
  - o Researchers Michele Gelfand and Anu Realo conducted a study to see whether culture influenced negotiation process and outcomes. Were individualists more competitive and less willing to exchange information or make concessions? In a study of 102 undergraduate students, the answer was generally no, but that's not the whole story.

  - o In the study, the researchers manipulated whether the negotiators would be accountable for the outcome of the negotiation. In the high-accountability condition, participants were told that they would have to justify their negotiated agreements to a manager. In the no-accountability condition, participants were told that no one would evaluate their negotiations.

  - o When both negotiators were individualists, they were indeed less cooperative but only in the high-accountability condition. In effect, the individualists chose to act less cooperatively when they knew they would be evaluated. In contrast, collectivist pairs exhibited higher levels of cooperation when they knew they would be evaluated. When people know that others are watching, they are more likely to behave consistently with cultural expectations.

o These results offer an interesting recommendation for increasing collaboration in high-profile negotiations. In the individualistic United States, high-profile negotiations are likely to result in posturing and conflict. But such negotiations might be more collaborative if they are conducted privately and if the results are revealed in a general rather than a detailed fashion. The opposite would be true when the parties are from collectivist countries. In those countries, making the negotiations public and clearly revealing the results should lead to more cooperation.

Game Theory

- The Gelfand and Realo study focused on pairs of negotiators who were similar in their approaches, but obviously, that situation doesn't always hold true. What if a collectivist who relies on soft tactics and an individualist who leans toward hard tactics come together at the negotiating table?

- Early research on game theory in economics offers some insight into what one might do in such situations. Game theory is the study of strategic decision making that analyzes conflict and competition between decision makers. The Prisoner's Dilemma is the most well-known and comprehensively studied example of this type of game.
  o In this game, two players take on the roles of members of a criminal gang that have been arrested and imprisoned; they cannot communicate. Because the police don't have enough evidence to convict both on the principal charge, they realize that they might have to settle for a lesser charge and a prison term of only a year for each. The police offer both prisoners a deal: If one testifies against the partner, he or she will go free, while the partner will get three years in prison on the main

charge. However, if both prisoners testify against each other, both will get two years in prison.

o   When this game is played under most situations, betrayal is a common outcome. Not trusting the unknown party, each prisoner is unwilling to risk getting three years while the other goes free; thus, both people testify and get two years.

- In an iterated version of this classic game, the two players get multiple opportunities to collaborate or betray. In this case, it is more likely that some pairs will collaborate. Based on years of research, the tit-for-tat strategy has emerged as the best approach in this version. Effectively, you start nice and defect only after the other party does, in retaliation. After a defection, you should proceed with a forgiving attitude and return to being nice.

- How can the tit-for-tat strategy be applied in real-life negotiation contexts? Start with an effort to pursue a principle-based strategy. If it becomes clear that you are dealing with someone is focused on positions, alternate between using hard and soft influence tactics depending on what your negotiating partner has done most recently.

Application: Successful Negotiations

- At the beginning of this lecture, we looked at the case of two doctors interested in obtaining rare fruit to save lives. As it turns out, the information provided in this classic business case notes that Dr. Jones needs only the juice of the fruit, while Dr. Roland needs only the rind. In fact, both parties can get what they need from the fruit, and the negotiation can focus on how they can collaborate to implement this win-win solution. The point of this teaching exercise is to encourage participants to explore and discuss the principles that underlie their requests.

- The next time you enter a negotiation in which you hope for a mutually agreeable solution, inquire into the other party's interests. Experiment with using such words as "we" and "us" to see whether doing so creates a difference in the other party's approach.

- The next time you hear an argument, listen carefully. Are the parties being clear about their interests, or are they caught up in defensive posturing and accusations? Don't intervene (unless necessary), but imagine what you might do if you were one of the parties. How could you break the cycle and begin a conversation about principles rather than positions?

Suggested Reading

Cohen, *You Can Negotiate Anything*.

Fisher, Ury, and Patton, *Getting to Yes*.

Activities to Try

1. The next time you enter a negotiation in which you hope for a mutually agreeable solution, inquire into the other party's interests. Experiment with using such words as "we" and "us" to see whether that tactic creates a difference in the other party's approach.

2. The next time you hear an argument between two parties, listen carefully. Are they being clear about their interests, or are they caught up in defensive posturing and accusations? Imagine what you might do if you were one of the parties. How could you break the cycle and begin a conversation about principles rather than positions?

Developing Negotiation Skills
Lecture 11—Transcript

Herb Cohen, the author of the classic bestselling book *You Can Negotiate Anything*, calls the world a giant negotiating table. When I read this, I imagine looking across a long table at all the faces of people I work with, my department chair, my dean, members of committees I run, my students, my community partners, my research colleagues in Australia, United Kingdom, Norway, my banker, real estate agent, cell phone sales person, and the faces of all the people that I play with but still negotiate about what and when to play, friends, spouse, kids. It's truly a large table. And rightfully so. Negotiations happen around us all the time. Some proceed quickly and easily; others drag on, and everyone gets angry. Getting what you deserve out of a negotiation, and having everyone walk away satisfied, is a specific application of influence. Like all influence situations, doing it well is a combination of art and science that can have profound implications for you, your coworkers, and even society at large.

In this lecture, I want to talk about how you can use influence successfully in negotiation settings. By successful, I don't just mean that you get what you want, but that you and your negotiating partner walk away feeling satisfied that the results are fair. How can we get to fair as an outcome of negotiation? Let me walk you through a classic negotiation exercise, one that is used in business school, classrooms, all around the world.

Imagine you are sitting in an executive training program, and the professor divides the class into two groups. Your group is shepherded into a separate room and given a briefing sheet to read. Here is a summary. You are Dr. Jones, a biological research scientist employed by a pharmaceutical company. You have recently developed a synthetic chemical useful for curing a disease contracted by pregnant women. If not dealt with in the first four weeks of pregnancy, the disease causes serious damage to the unborn child. Unfortunately, the serum is made from a very rare fruit. Only about 4,000 were grown in the world this season. You have recently been told that a Mr. Cardoza, a South American fruit exporter, has 3,000 of these fruit. If you could obtain all 3,000, then you could make enough serum from the juice to both cure all the present victims and inoculate all remaining pregnant women. You have a budget. It's $250,000.

Of course, you aren't the only one seeking those fruit. One Dr. Roland is also urgently hoping to get these fruit from Mr. Cardoza. Dr. Roland is employed by a competing pharmaceutical company. Roland has been working on biological warfare research for the past several years. Before approaching Cardoza, you decide to talk to Dr. Roland.

With that briefing, you walk back into your classroom and are paired with another student who plays the role of Dr. Roland. How do you begin your negotiation? What do you say, and what do you not say in trying to secure the 3,000 very rare fruit? If you're like many students, you begin with a somewhat guarded but very passionate explanation of why your need is so great. You are, after all, trying to help prevent birth defects. To your surprise, Dr. Roland also offers a plea for the fruit and has an equally great cause. She is actually trying to create an antidote to a neurological toxin that is leaking from a chemical weapons site and threatening innocent lives. So who gets the fruit? Many negotiating pairs have a hard time reaching agreement, as it turns out that each needs more than half of the fruit for a meaningful cause. Splitting them in half means that neither party gets what it needs.

There is a surprising resolution to this case, but I'm not going to give it to you right now. Instead, I'm going to wait until the end of the lecture to revisit Dr. Jones and Dr. Roland. In the meantime, I'd like to explore some of the strategies that the doctors might use to influence each other in their negotiation. Influence and negotiation have much in common, but they are not precisely the same thing. There's an important difference between negotiation settings and the many different examples of influence we've used earlier in the course. In a negotiation, people generally come together with the express purpose of reaching an agreement, and thus it's a concentrated time and space within which a variety of different influence tactics get applied. And it's a time when people are acutely aware that they're being subjected to influence, so they are often guarded.

In their book, *Getting to Yes*, Roger Fisher and William Ury identify two broad negotiation strategies, which they call principle-based negotiation and position-based negotiation. Fisher and Ury also describe three criteria that we should use to determine whether a negotiation tactic is successful. First, it results in a settlement that is agreeable to both parties. Two, it's efficient, and three, the parties are willing to work together again. When these three things happen, we'll call it a win-win; both parties walk away having won. So the question becomes, which general strategy, principle-based or position-based, is more conducive to achieving a win-win outcome? Let's see each one in operation.

Let's start with position-based negotiation. Position-based negotiation occurs when each party focuses on a concrete position that must be obtained. In the case of the rare fruit and your role as Dr. Jones, you might make Dr. Roland an offer, asking her not to seek the fruit if you give her $100,000. That's effectively a cost of $100,000 for all 4,000 fruit produced worldwide. You might offer this knowing that you actually have $250,000 to spend and only need 3,000 fruit. You've left yourself wiggle room to be talked down or influenced into paying a bit more or buying a bit less. But in the end, you know you won't settle for any position that costs more than $250,000 and results in fewer than 3,000 fruit in hand. You are focused on the numbers.

Back in the real world, you might use the same approach when trying to buy a car. You might refuse to pay any more than $10,000 for a used car that you've been looking at. In the case of home buying, it may be that a seller refuses to pay any of the settlement costs, and focuses all the negotiation on making sure that all cash costs of the sale are covered by the buyer. If a young man walks into a store and offers a lowball price for a refrigerator, saying "If you can't sell this to me for $450, then I'm leaving," he's using position-based negotiating.

In each case, a fixed, concrete monetary position is established that leads the person to see any outcome of the negotiation as either a win, I got what I wanted, or a loss, I failed. So position-based negotiation also has been called a win-lose approach. When people adopt this approach, you can inadvertently cut off potentially creative solutions, and one person almost always walks away frustrated. The end result is often, although certainly not always, no deal.

I've seen that happen in house buying. When my wife and I made a very good monetary offer on a house in our neighborhood, we attached a contingency. The seller refused the contingency, and we countered by giving in even more in terms of convenience of closing date and cost. The seller still refused, focused solely on that single contingency. We decided to build our own version of that house a bit further down the street. Because of the seller's sole focus on a single position—no contingency—they did not sell the house for over a year. We were nearly ready to move into our new house when they finally sold. The influence tactics used in position-based negotiation can vary, but they easily fall into hard tactics, like pressure. When you get caught up in a particular number or issue, then you may find yourself frustrated that the other party won't just give in, and your frustration comes out in loudly stated demands or even ultimatums.

Let's contrast this with principle-based negotiation. This approach involves exploring each party's underlying interests and seeking solutions that are mutually beneficial. Rather than pressure, a focus on interest pushes people to soft influence tactics, rational argument, inspiration, and exchange. In the case of the home we tried to purchase, it would have been helpful if we had understood why the sellers were so averse to that particular contingency, and if they knew why we wanted to have it in place. Perhaps there was a creative way that both of our concerns could have been addressed.

Real-world examples of principle-based negotiation occur all the time. The one that I'd like to focus on involves two electricity providers on the West Coast in the United States. One of the providers, the Bonneville Power Administration, is a federal nonprofit agency that markets wholesale power from 31 hydroelectric projects in the Pacific Northwest. The other provider, Southern California Edison, relies on nuclear, hydro, and coal-fired facilities to deliver energy to customers in Central and Southern California. In the early 1990s, each organization had environmental problems. Bonneville had problems with their hydroelectric plants reducing water flow too much. To make sure water was available to generate electricity for heating in the fall and winter months, Bonneville would block water behind their dams during spring and summer. The end result was enough electricity year-round, but dangerously low water flow for salmon migration during spring and summer.

It was looking like a win-lose situation, with the salmon, environmentalists, and the local fishing lobby all on the losing side.

Meanwhile, further south along the U.S. coast, Southern California Edison had problems with their coal plants adding smog to the already murky Los Angeles skies. They were looking for ways to cut back on how much coal they burned, but they also didn't want to create power shortages. So they started to negotiate with other power suppliers in order to purchase power in the spring and summer when hot weather leads to peak energy demands in Southern California. Doing so would allow them to reduce coal burning at those times.

It turns out that there was a solution to both Bonneville and Edison's problems that only required a creative mindset and a little bit of trust. By allowing extra water release in the spring and summer and generating surplus power at that time, Bonneville was able to lend that power to Edison. Edison then reduced its use of coal-fired plants during that time, which reduced emissions that contribute to smog, especially in the hot months. Later in the year, when Bonneville no longer had enough water behind their dams to spin their turbines and the summer smog had started to dissipate, Edison could fire up its plants and return the electricity they borrowed from Bonneville. In the end, this cost effectively no money, and the environmental benefits up and down the West Coast were extensive. Here we have a classic example of principle-based negotiation. The parties arrived at a creative, win-win solution. If the companies had been solely focused on money when they started negotiating, they could have fought for months over pricing. Instead, by bringing to the table environmental concerns and the question of timing, they were able to create a truly win-win solution.

What leads people to come together with an approach to be creative and help each other solve problems? We have to remember that behind these big company names are managers with past history negotiating, with personalities, and with biases. The ATTiC model reminds us that these characteristics of agents play a role in what influence tactics they'll use. Research indicates that one of the most important agent characteristics leading to principle-based negotiation is having confidence. Research by Brandon Sullivan, Kathleen O'Connor, and Ethan Burris suggests that people who have confidence that they can establish rapport, find trade-offs, and exchange concessions tend to be much more likely to begin negotiations with the principle, win-win approach.

As with any effort to build confidence, the best advice I can offer is to practice. You can build confidence by doing further reading and reflection and then applying principle-based tactics anytime you can, with family, with friends, and even with that annoying mattress sales person who keeps pushing the pillow-top model. That will help you gain confidence, which in turn will enable you to seek win-win solutions in more complex negotiations. The ATTiC model also reminds us that context matters. In the case of negotiations, a turbulent past history that creates animosity and reduces trust makes it unlikely that creative solutions will emerge. If Bonneville Power Authority and Southern California Edison had had prior conflicts in the courts, then executives from the firms might not have trusted each other enough to agree. And what they agreed upon was the very first environmentally-focused power exchange ever.

A more personal setting in which conflict and lack of trust plays out is in divorce proceedings. Couples who are saddled with frustration and lack of trust are usually unwilling to openly discuss issues, to consider any concessions, and to propose win-win solutions. So confidence and a trusting relationship help lead to principle-based negotiating and to win-win outcomes. Let's return to position-based negotiation and see how the ATTiC model helps us understand when it occurs. Beginning with context, research suggests that time pressure can contribute to the use of position-based negotiation. Under pressure, it's more difficult to take the time to exchange information, to consider alternatives, and ultimately find a mutually beneficial solution.

Technology may also play an important contextual role, leading to position-based negotiation. In a study conducted at Tel Aviv University, researchers found that people negotiating via email used fewer soft and more hard tactics than those working face-to-face. So if you're negotiating via technology, such as trying to buy a car online, you'll be more likely to see hard tactics pop up. These may help you get a good deal today or might help the dealer take advantage of you, but keep in mind the trade-off for future business.

If you want to have a good working relationship in the future, soft tactics associated with principle-based negotiation should be your choice and the choice of the business you're working with.

So we've considered context and noted how time pressure and technology can lead to win-lose approaches to negotiation. Now, let's talk about the agent characteristics that are associated with this approach. A personal characteristic that may lead to a preference for position-based negotiation is competitiveness. In the United States, we often point to lawyers as the quintessential example. In the U.S., legal education often socializes law students to be competitive to the point of aggressiveness. While not all lawyers in the U.S. are like this, when the educational system attracts competitive students and further develops argumentative approaches to winning, the end result is a tendency for lawyers to adopt a style that is position- rather than principle-based.

If you think I am over-generalizing, let me quote an article written by law professor Andrea Kupfer Schneider and published in the Harvard Negotiation Law Review:

> "Few law students are afraid of being too adversarial ... Given the choice between being too soft and too hard, most lawyers would opt for being too hard ... Law school provides an opportunity to modify this trend, but ... the teaching methodology still used by some first-year professors appears quite adversarial to students ... It is combat."

But the news is not all bad for lawyers. In the same article, professor Schneider goes on to report survey results from over 700 lawyers in the Milwaukee and Chicago areas. Results revealed that lawyers generally believe in being principled in negotiations. In other words, they believe that seeking win-win solutions and cooperating are more effective than competing and pushing to maximize settlements. So there's good reason to hope that attitudes are changing.

In addition to competitiveness, what other agent characteristics might lead one to choose position-based negotiation over principle-based approach?

What about culture? In an earlier lecture we discussed the difference between individualists and collectivists. Individualists are concerned with their own goals and interests and place them above the interests of the group. Collectivists, on the other hand, are concerned with the goals and interests of the group and place them above their own interests as individuals. Given these definitions it might seem obvious that individualists would be more prone to position-based negotiation. The truth is a bit more complicated.

Michele Gelfand, from the University of Maryland, and Anu Realo, from the University of Tartu in Estonia, conducted a study to see whether culture influenced negotiation process and outcomes. Were individualists more competitive, less willing to exchange information and make concessions? In a study of 102 undergraduate students, the answer was generally no, but that's not the whole story. In this study, the researchers manipulated whether the negotiators would be accountable for the outcome of the negotiation. In the high-accountability condition, participants were told that they would have to justify their negotiated agreement to a manager. In the no-accountability condition, participants were told that no one would evaluate their negotiation outcome. When both negotiators were individualists, they were, indeed, less cooperative, but only in the high-accountability condition. In effect, the individualists chose to act less cooperatively when they knew they would be subsequently evaluated. Similarly, pairs who were collectivistic exhibited higher levels of cooperation when they knew they would be evaluated. So when people know that others are watching, they are more likely to behave consistently with the cultural expectation that they hold.

These results offer an interesting recommendation for making high-profile negotiations more collaborative. In the United States, which is filled with individualists, high-profile negotiations are more likely to result in posturing and conflict. In the U.S., negotiations might be more collaborative if they are conducted privately and the results revealed in a general fashion, rather than a detailed fashion, where the point-by-point ideas might be laid out. The opposite would be true when the parties are from countries with many collectivist citizens, like Venezuela, Pakistan, or South Korea. In these countries, having negotiations be more public and the results clearly enumerated, should lead to more cooperation.

In the Gelfand and Realo study, and in our discussion of principle-based negotiation, we focused on pairs of negotiators who were similar in their approach. But clearly this doesn't always happen. What if a collectivist who relies on soft tactics and an individualist who leans towards hard tactics come together at a negotiating table? Perhaps more pointedly, what about a situation in which you are trying to be collaborative and the person you are negotiating with is doing nothing but playing hard ball? If you are repeatedly making concessions in the situation and they're never reciprocated, then it does not make sense to continue. The end result won't be a win-win solution, just a miserable outcome for you.

Early research on game theory in economics offers some insight into what one might do in such situations. Game theory is the study of strategic decision making that analyzes conflict and competition between decision makers. You may have heard of the Prisoner's Dilemma; it's the best known, and probably best studied, example of this type of game. The Prisoner's Dilemma game begins with the following setup. Two members of a criminal gang are arrested and imprisoned. Each prisoner is in solitary confinement with no means of speaking to or exchanging messages with the other. The police know they don't have enough evidence to convict the pair on the principal charge. So they plan to sentence both to a year in prison on a lesser charge. Simultaneously, the police offer each prisoner a deal. If he testifies against his partner, he will go free, while the partner will get three years in prison on the main charge.

Oh, yes, there's a catch. If both prisoners testify against each other, both will be sentenced to two years in jail. When this game is played under most situations, betrayal is a common outcome. Not trusting the other party, not knowing what they're going to do, boy, a person is unwilling to risk getting three years while the other goes free. So, both people testify and get two years in jail.

Another version of this classic game is the iterated version, where two players get multiple opportunities to collaborate or betray. In this case, it's more likely that at least some pairs will begin to collaborate. What is the best strategy in this game to maximize your outcome, if you're playing it with the prison version to spend the least time in jail? Based on years of research, the tit-for-tat strategy has emerged as the best approach. This effectively means that you start off nice, and then only defect after the other party does, effectively retaliating. But then you should proceed with a forgiving attitude and return to being nice.

How might the tit-for-tat strategy be used in real-life negotiation contexts? Well, you could start with an effort to pursue principle-based strategies. But if it's clear that you're dealing with someone who's focused on positions, you should try to collect as much information as possible. Prepare yourself so you understand exactly what their limitations are. If, for example, you know what a car dealership paid for a car, having read a car buying guide, then you can counter tit-for-tat in a manner that gives you great possibility for a good outcome. When the salesperson says, "Boy, I can't let this car go for less than $19,000," you can counter with, because you did your research, "I understand that this car generally goes to you as the dealer for $18,000, and I am more comfortable with a $500 profit on your end. But if the profit goes to $1000, I have to tell you, I feel like I'm getting a bad deal." Knowing a reasonable figure to put back in play as part of this tit-for-tat exchange, you can have a real advantage that may help you get a good deal.

Drawing on work by Roger Fisher and William Ury, I've presented the case for principle-based negotiation. It is fundamentally sound and should be your preferred approach to negotiation. It's more likely to happen if you're confident and hold back on any competitive instinct that you have. If you find yourself in a situation with someone who's quite competitive, then you can adopt the logic of the tit-for-tat strategy and alternate between hard and soft tactics depending on what your negotiating partner has done most recently.

Let's return now to the situation of Dr. Roland and Dr. Jones, our opening case. Recall that each was interested in obtaining all 3,000 of the rare fruit to help save lives. How can an agreement be reached that benefits both parties? Is there a principle-based solution? There is, if the right information is put on the negotiating table. Let's revisit the information given to each party. Dr. Jones was told, "If you could obtain all 3,000, you could make enough serum from the juice to cure all the present victims and inoculate others." Dr. Roland, whose instructions I did not read, was given somewhat different information. "If you get all 3,000, you could make enough of the chemical from the fruit rind to neutralize all of the deadly gas." If Dr. Jones indicates as part of the negotiation that all he needs is the juice of the fruit, and Dr. Roland indicates that all she needs is the rind, then it becomes clear that 3,000 fruit can be had by both and the negotiation can begin to focus on how they can collaborate to make this win-win solution come to life.

Clearly, this is a case designed to have a relatively straightforward win-win solution. We do not always find ourselves in a situation where things work out so cleanly. But the point of the teaching exercise is that you won't know whether you're in such a situation unless you explore and discuss the principles that underlie your requests.

As always, let's end the lecture with two things you can try. First, the next time you enter a negotiation where you hope for a mutually agreeable solution, inquire into the other party's interests. Use words like we and us, and see whether it creates a difference in the other party's approach. We discussed reciprocation in an earlier lecture, and your efforts to put forward a principle-based approach, to think about this as a collective endeavor, to seek a win-win, may well elicit the same from the other party.

Second, the next time you hear an argument between two parties, listen carefully. Are the parties actually being clear about their interests, or are they caught up in defensive posturing and accusations? Don't intervene, unless you're the parent, or it's your job, but imagine what you might do if you were one of the parties. How could you break the cycle and begin a conversation about principles rather than positions?

In our next lecture, we will conclude our course with a discussion of leaders. To be successful, leaders have to do all the things we've talked about so far in this course, not just use influence tactics, but negotiate, sell, build positive impressions, and of course, make speeches. I'll present theory and stories just showing how some of the world's most amazing leaders make it all happen. I'll end by trying to convince you that none of this is reserved for an elite few. These are things you too can do.

Becoming a Transformational Leader
Lecture 12

In 1994, Ray Anderson, the late CEO of Interface, Inc., a global carpet company, asked his employees to commit to transforming the company into a model of a sustainable, green business. Between 1996 and 2008, Interface reduced its greenhouse gas emissions by 82 percent and its fossil fuel use by 60 percent, while dramatically increasing sales and doubling profits. Anderson was a transformational leader. He used his formal position, his passion, and influence to change the way business was done. In this lecture, we'll discuss leadership and influence, specifically what differentiates such leaders as Anderson from more traditional corporate managers. We'll also explore what Anderson's example has to teach us about becoming influential leaders in our own right.

Leadership: Theory and Research

- For many years, leadership research focused on what has been called the great man theory. Scholars posed the question: What traits make some people great leaders and others poor leaders or not leaders at all? They found some key differences between those who emerge as leaders and those who do not. But more recent studies have discovered something that matters even more than individual traits. What matters most, according to the latest research, is the nature of the relationship between the leader and his or her followers.

- In a major synthesis of prior research, a 2011 article in the journal *Personnel Psychology* examined different types of leadership and their relationships with leadership outcomes, such as follower satisfaction with the leader, follower motivation, follower job performance, and, ultimately, performance of the group or organization of which followers were a part. The researchers, Tim Judge and Ron Piccolo, found that the best predictor of these outcomes was a particular style of leadership called transformational leadership.

- The concept of transformational leadership comes from a political historian, James MacGregor Burns, who has written a number of books on presidential history. In a book about leadership more generally, Burns argued that different leaders develop different types of relationships with their followers. Specifically, he distinguished between transactional and transformational leaders.

  o Transactional leadership occurs when the relationship between followers and leaders is based on exchange that meets each party's needs. Followers do what the leader wants in exchange for something they want, such as to keep their jobs or to earn bonuses.

  o Transformational leadership occurs when the relationship between followers and leaders is based on influence through values and ideals. Burns cites Franklin Roosevelt as an example of a transformational leader. In his efforts to sell his New Deal programs to Congress, Roosevelt sought to connect them to the U.S. Constitution and the core value of freedom. By offering these connections, Roosevelt was building a relationship with followers based on higher-order principles and ideals.

The Four I's of Transformational Leadership

- Professors Bernie Bass and Bruce Avolio extended Burns's ideas to the study of business leaders. Their research suggests that transformational leadership has four dimensions: idealized influence, inspirational motivation, intellectual stimulation, and individualized consideration.

  o Idealized influence occurs when leaders accept that they are role models and behave in admirable ways. Such leaders display passion and conviction and, thus, appeal to followers on an emotional level.

  o Inspirational motivation requires that the leader develop and promote a vision that captures people's hearts and minds. The vision must be positive and provide meaning to the hard work that is being asked of followers.

o Intellectual stimulation requires that the leader challenge the status quo and involve followers in developing ideas. Leaders who do this well engage their followers in pushing forward their shared cause.

o Individualized consideration requires that the leader listen to followers, acknowledge their concerns and needs, and support them.

- How did Ray Anderson make use of these four I's of transformational leadership?

  o Instead of motivating his employees by offering to share profits with them or arguing that their jobs were at stake if they couldn't reduce the company's greenhouse emissions, Anderson used inspirational motivation. He appealed to the lofty goals of saving the planet for the next generation and finding better ways to do business.

  o Anderson used idealized influence by serving as a role model for his Mission Zero. He personally committed time and money to the efforts to alter his business and spent time outside of business writing and speaking about the environment. His personal behavior was a critical element in his overall attempt to influence his employees.

  o We can also see how Anderson used intellectual stimulation: He didn't tell his employees how to make the business environmentally friendly but challenged them to figure it out! He had high expectations of his employees and turned over considerable decision-making power to them to test out new ideas.

  o Finally, Anderson displayed individualized consideration by recognizing people for their ideas and efforts.

- Transformational leaders do exactly what the label suggests: They transform people and, through those people, help build a better world. But this should not be interpreted to mean that transactional leaders are not useful.

- o In their studies, Judge and Piccolo found a few outcomes that were higher for transactional than for transformational leaders, including followers' job satisfaction and job performance of the leader.

- o These results point to the idea that transactional leaders may be quite effective in helping their employees understand what to do, with the clarity improving satisfaction. These leaders may also be better at doing what is required of them in their core job requirements. Transformational leaders are not necessarily bad at doing these things, but it's easy to picture a transformational leader focusing on a grand vision at the expense of operational details.

Developing Transformational Leaders
- Julian Barling, of Queen's University, and his colleagues conducted a study to explore the question or whether transformational leaders are born or made. These researchers provided transformational leadership training to a group of bank managers and then tested whether their leadership behaviors and the performance of their branches changed.
  - o Employees of trained managers showed increases in commitment to the bank, and they worked harder, generating more sales than they had before their managers were trained. There were no changes in employees of non-trained managers.

  - o These results offer a clear indication that we can all become at least somewhat more transformational in our approaches to leading others.

- John Antonakis and his colleagues at the University of Lausanne conducted research leading to the same conclusion. For their study, researchers videotaped 41 business students giving speeches. They then trained these students in methods to become more transformational in their speaking style, such as using stories, concrete symbols, and vivid language that elicits emotion. When the same students were taped after training, they were found to much more engaging and convincing by a group of more than 100 independent raters.

- Professor Stefani Yorges and her colleagues tested whether leaders who had shown a willingness to sacrifice for their beliefs would be seen as more influential. Yorges found that people who had sacrificed in the past are more likely to be given the benefit of the doubt with regard to motives. This may explain the success of so many military figures in politics: They sacrificed to serve their country, and as a result, their motives are less open to criticism.

Nelson Mandela

- Among those whose past sacrifice serves as a strong foundation for subsequent efforts to influence and persuade, Nelson Mandela comes immediately to mind. As a leading figure in the African National Congress (ANC), Mandela stood in opposition to the racist apartheid system since its inception in 1948. Initially, he favored nonviolent tactics, but in the face of ongoing repression, he changed his mind. In 1955, he claimed publicly that the ANC had "no alternative to armed and violent resistance."

- This decision and his subsequent actions led to Mandela's arrest in 1962 and the banning of the ANC as a political party. In 1964, Mandela was found guilty of conspiracy to overthrow the government and was sentenced to life in prison. In total, Mandela spent 27 years in prison, where he suffered permanent damage to his eyesight and caught tuberculosis. But he also remained involved in politicking and continued to build his reputation and to learn.

- In 1990, the new white leader of South Africa, Frederik de Klerk, decided that apartheid was unsustainable, and he met with Mandela. After the meeting, de Klerk freed Mandela unconditionally and lifted the ban on the ANC. Much of the ensuing two years was spent in formal negotiation between de Klerk's government and the ANC as they attempted to dismantle apartheid. A free election was set for April 1994, and Mandela won the presidency; he then began work on what many consider to be his lasting legacy.

- Although Mandela had embraced violence earlier in his life, he came out strongly for national reconciliation. He used inspirational language and set himself up as a role model. He referred to South Africa as the "Rainbow Nation" and brought whites into his governing cabinet, at the same time encouraging blacks to support the national rugby team.

- As Yorges found, sacrifice makes leaders even more influential. In Mandela's case, he sacrificed nearly everything to the advancement of political rights for blacks. Following the collapse of apartheid, there were some who called for war and justice by jailing the oppressors. Mandela, however, had the higher goal of reconciliation in mind and was able to convince his countrymen to join him in pursuit of that higher goal. Were it not for Mandela's transformational leadership, South Africa may well have descended

As president, Nelson Mandela used inspirational motivation by focusing attention on symbols of unity, and he used idealized influence by modeling forgiveness of those who had held him prisoner for so many years.

into civil war, rather than move peacefully forward toward national unity and economic prosperity.

- Not many of us have sacrificed in the way that Nelson Mandela sacrificed, but it's still possible to draw on your own history to convince others that your motives are good.

Application: Using Influence for Transformation

- Consider an issue or cause that is personally important to you. Are you passionate about the need for more public land in your town? Do you think local property taxes are too high? Does the local animal shelter need a new facility? In each case, there is an opportunity for someone like you to be transformative. Choose your cause, reach out to others, build relationships based on common values and interests, establish a shared vision, and mobilize people to bring about change.

- As an alternative to acting as a formal spokesperson for your cause, design and plan an influence campaign. To mobilize people's hearts and minds, help decide on the ideals and symbols, stories and figureheads that will win people over. By mastering the underlying mechanisms of influence, you are now better prepared to be a force for positive change in your home, your business, and your community.

Suggested Reading

Anderson, *Mid-Course Correction.*

Bass and Avolio, *Improving Organizational Effectiveness through Transformational Leadership.*

Burns, *Leadership.*

Mandela, *Long Walk to Freedom.*

1. Consider an issue or cause that is personally important to you. Once you choose your cause, reach out to others, build relationships based on common values and interests, establish a shared vision, and mobilize people to make change happen.

2. Prepare the influence campaign that must accompany your group's efforts. You may not be the one to deliver the speeches, but you can help design the components—the ideals and symbols—that will inspire others.

Becoming a Transformational Leader
Lecture 12—Transcript

"Do no harm to the environment and take nothing from the earth that is not easily renewed by the earth!" This was the mantra of Ray Anderson, the late CEO of Interface Inc., a global carpet company. In 1994, Anderson stood before the employees of his company and posed this challenge to them. He stated the mantra and asked them to commit to what he called Mission Zero, a mission to transform their company into a model of sustainable, green business with zero environmental footprint. But how could a single man, running a synthetic carpet company, a product largely created by oil, transform his product and his business practices so they did no harm to the environment? Anderson's story is a great example of how one man's personal transformation can revolutionize an entire industry.

At the age of 60, Anderson read Paul Hawken's book, "*The Ecology of Commerce: A Declaration of Sustainability*." The book convinced him that his business was pillaging the earth, and that as a result, he was not a hero of industry, but a villain who was robbing from the next generation. Rather than take this as criticism, Anderson took it as a challenge, and he extended that challenge to his employees. He challenged them to work together and transform how they did business by using technology to climb Mount Sustainability. Throughout the mission, or climb, as he called it, he set difficult goals for his company, encouraged and supported employees as they experimented with new technology, and used inspiring imagery of climbing a summit and transforming industry. In other words, he used influence to alter his company and set new standards for how businesses should be run.

What progress did Anderson's company make in their climb up Mount Sustainability? Well, between 1996 and 2008, Interface Inc. reduced its greenhouse gas emissions by 82 percent, while dramatically increasing sales and doubling profits. Interface also reduced fossil fuel use by 60 percent per unit of production, and the company managed to cut water usage by 75 percent. It's hard to get your head around these accomplishments, because it's hard to imagine how so many good things could come from this effort. Interface has grown substantially. It makes more money for its owners and investors than ever before, and at the same time, it has dramatically, dramatically improved in how ecologically friendly it is.

By all accounts, Anderson is a leader. He used his formal position, and his passion, and lots of influence techniques to get his employees to change what they were doing, and he didn't stop there. He wrote two books and appeared in numerous interviews, was profiled in many newspaper and magazine articles, and even spoke a few years before his death at a 2009 TED conference. In his talk, he summarized his philosophy, his story, and the company's accomplishments. He also discussed how his employees were embracing higher purpose in their work lives. What this means is that Anderson didn't stop his work at the doors of his company; he leveraged its success to become an active and effective spokesperson throughout the business world.

In this lecture we will discuss leadership and influence, specifically what differentiates leaders like Ray Anderson from more traditional corporate managers. And then, we'll explore what Anderson's example has to teach us about becoming influential leaders in our own right. Let's start with a quick review of some theory and research on leadership.

For many years, leadership research focused on what has been called the great man theory. Scholars posed the question, What traits make some people great leaders and others poor leaders or not leaders at all? They tested whether leaders were smarter, taller, more sociable, more likeable, and so on. What they found was that there are some key differences, on average, between those who emerge as leaders and those who do not. But, more recent studies have discovered something that matters even more than individual traits. What matters most, according to the latest research, is the nature of the relationship between the leader and her followers.

In a major synthesis of prior research, a 2011 article in the journal *Personnel Psychology* examines different types of leadership and their relationships with leadership outcomes. What do I mean by leadership outcomes? Well, they include follower satisfaction with the leader, follower motivation, follower job performance, follower judgment about the leader's effectiveness, and, ultimately, the performance of the group or organization that followers are a part of. The researchers, Tim Judge and Ron Piccolo, found that the best predictor of these outcomes overall was a particular style of leadership called transformational leadership. The concept of transformational leadership comes from a political historian, James MacGregor Burns. Burns, Professor Emeritus at Williams College, has written a number of books on presidential history, and received a Pulitzer for his book on President Franklin Delano Roosevelt. In a subsequent book about leadership, more generally, Burns argued that different leaders develop different types of relationships with their followers. Specifically, he distinguished between transactional and transformational leaders.

Transactional leadership occurs when the relationship between followers and leaders is based on exchange that meets each party's needs. Followers do what the leader wants in exchange for something they want. Burns cites the stoic philosopher Epictetus, who wrote, "No one is afraid of Caesar himself, but he is afraid of death, loss of property, prison, and disenfranchisement. Nor does anyone love Caesar himself … but we love wealth." In other words, the relationship between the Senators and Caesar was based on influence through rewards and punishment. You do what Caesar wants, and you get what you want. In everyday work life, you see this play out with supervisors who try to influence their employees to work harder by threat, pick up the pace or lose your job; or by reward, if you pick up the pace, you'll earn a bonus. That's transactional leadership.

Transformational leadership is different. It occurs when the relationship between followers and leaders is based on influence through values and ideals. Burns uses many examples of this type of leadership in his book, including Franklin Delano Roosevelt, who established a New Deal for the American people, and Mahatma Gandhi, who established the first Indian state by freeing his people from the British Empire.

Let's look at Roosevelt for a minute. Roosevelt was certainly a great tactical politician; he was not above trading favors to get votes. But when it came time to sell his New Deal to Congress and the American people, he spent a great time of time and effort thinking through how to inspire support for this enormous initiative. Roosevelt argued, "Necessitous men are not free men," which connected the concept of freedom to proposed programs to create jobs, medical care, and retirement income. He also referred to these programs as a New Deal, akin to a second Bill of Rights. Roosevelt was trying to inspire support of these programs by connecting them to the original U.S. constitution and to the core value of freedom. By offering these connections, Roosevelt was building a relationship with followers based on higher-order principles and ideals. That's the essence of transformational leadership.

You might ask whether the concept of transformational leadership applies outside of politics. The answer is absolutely yes. For example, many business scholars have been influenced by Burns' book. In particular, Bernie Bass and Bruce Avolio took Burns' ideas and extended them to the study of business leaders. They went so far as to write survey instruments and collect detailed data about the different aspects of leadership and its consequences. Bass and Avolio suggest that transformational leadership has four dimensions, idealized influence, inspirational motivation, intellectual stimulation, and individualized consideration. This model has been studied extensively and has been labeled the four I's of transformational leadership. Let's discuss each of these dimensions.

Idealized influence occurs when leaders accept that they are role models and behave in admirable ways. Leaders like this display passion and conviction, and so appeal to their followers on an emotional level. Inspirational motivation requires that the leader develop and promote a vision that captures people's hearts and minds. The vision must be positive and provide meaning to the hard work that's being asked of followers. Intellectual stimulation requires that the leader challenge the status quo and involve followers in developing ideas. Leaders who do this well engage their followers in pushing forward their shared cause. Finally, individualized consideration requires that the leader listen to her followers, acknowledge their concerns and needs, and support them.

To make these four I's of transformational leadership more concrete, let's revisit Ray Anderson. Anderson did not attempt to motivate his employees by saying, "If we cut expenses, I'll share profits with you," or by arguing that their jobs were at stake if they couldn't reduce the company's greenhouse emissions. Instead, Anderson used inspirational motivation by appealing to the lofty goal of saving the planet for the next generation, of finding new and better ways to do business. He was appealing not to their pocketbooks, but to their hearts, minds, and souls.

And Anderson used idealized influence as well; he was a role model for Mission Zero. He put his money where his mouth was. He personally committed a good deal of time and money to those efforts to alter his business. He spent a considerable amount of his time outside of the business writing and speaking about the environment, and when he built a vacation home later in his career, he built it using the most environmentally friendly technology at the time with the goal of zero environmental impact. In short, Anderson's personal behavior was a critical element in his overall attempt to influence his employees.

You can also see how Anderson used intellectual stimulation. He didn't tell his employees how to become environmentally friendly. He challenged them to figure it out. He had very high expectations, and he turned over considerable decision-making power to his employees so they could test out new ideas. And finally, Anderson displayed individualized consideration by recognizing people for their ideas and efforts. If you think about it, Anderson, when he was giving all these talks, could have taken all the credit for the initiatives and accomplishments of the company, but he regularly and routinely made mention of how important Hawken's thinking had been to Interface's transformation. In fact, Anderson and Hawken appear to have developed a great relationship based on mutual respect. Hawken even dedicated a revision of one of his classic books to Anderson.

So, in Ray Anderson we see how a leader who adopts the four I's can make a big difference in the world. Transformational leaders do exactly what the label suggests. They transform people, and through those people, help build a better world. None of this should be interpreted to mean that transactional leadership is not useful. As Burns himself notes in his book, both types of leadership are useful, and research bears this out as well. The study I mentioned earlier, by Tim Judge and Ron Piccolo, found that transactional leadership works too. In fact, a few outcomes were higher for transactional than transformational leaders, including the follower's job satisfaction and the job performance of the leader.

These results actually point to the idea that transactional leaders may be quite effective in helping their employees understand what to do, with the clarity improving subsequent satisfaction. These leaders may also be better at doing what is required of them in their core job requirements. Transformational leaders are not necessarily bad at doing these things, but it's easy to picture a transformational leader focusing on the grand vision at the expense of the everyday operational details. The value of transformational leaders, then, is not their ability to get basic things done, but in their capacity, to gather others together and lead change.

So we've distinguished between transactional and transformational leaders, and I've explained how people like Ray Anderson use the four I's to influence his company's employees and their industry peers. Now it's worth moving to the longstanding question of whether these types of leaders are born or made. Is transformational leadership something you're born into? Or is it a skill that we can develop and apply in our daily lives?

Queen's University's Julian Barling and his colleagues did a study that helps us answer this question. They provided transformational leadership training to a group of bank managers. To study whether the training worked, the researchers actually offered the training to half of the managers and tested to see whether their leadership behaviors changed and whether the performance of the branches where they work changed as well. They identified 20 branch managers working in the same bank and same region. Trained managers attended a workshop and received follow-up coaching sessions by an expert in transformational leadership.

The ultimate test of any leadership training should not be what happens to the leaders, but what happens to their employees. Employees of trained managers showed increases in commitment to the bank, and they worked harder, generating more sales than they had before their manager had been trained. There was no change in employees of non-trained managers. So using this ultimate test, this training, transformational leadership training, made a big difference for the bank branches.

These results offer a clear indication that while we may not all have a Ray Anderson hidden within us, we can all become more of a transformational leader in our approach dealing with others. The training that Barling and his colleagues used was not mystical. They explained to managers what it means to use idealized influence and inspirational motivation, and they asked those people to practice. I've worked with bank managers before, and they are not typically the most dynamic and persuasive group. So I have to say, if they can do it, you can too.

John Antonakis and his colleagues at the University of Lausanne conducted research leading to the same conclusion. For their study, the researchers videotaped 41 business students giving speeches. Then they trained the students how to be more transformational in their speaking style, using stories, symbols, and vivid language that elicits emotion. Remember our lecture on making speeches? These ideas should sound familiar. When the same students were taped after training, and those tapes were shown to over 100 independent raters, the speakers were found to be much more engaging and convincing. I find these results inspiring. I've worked with thousands of students over the years, and many wonder whether they can ever lead others. The answer is, if they choose to do so and are willing to learn, they and you absolutely can.

I hasten to add that some of my students don't necessarily enjoy managing others, so if that's the case, they should stop and think before they take a promotion with management responsibility. But whether an individual is in a management position or not, if they choose to do so they can lead. Let's remember that transformational leadership is about a relationship, not just about a single person standing on a stage giving a speech. And with a relationship, there are many complexities that arise. One of those complexities occurs in the interpretation of the leader's motives. When you see someone telling a story and setting herself up to be a symbol of change, appealing to the emotion of others to join her, what things go through your mind? One of the questions you might have is, why? Are this person's motives for leading really value-based and idealized, or are we being deceived by someone with a thirst for power and a Machiavellian personality?

Some people have personal histories that answer these questions. Stefani Yorges and her colleagues tested whether leaders who had shown a willingness to sacrifice for their beliefs would be seen as more influential.

What Yorges found is that past sacrifice does make a difference in how leaders are perceived. People who sacrificed in the past are more likely to be given the benefit of the doubt in their motives. This probably explains the success of so many military figures in political life; they sacrificed to serve their country, and as a result, their motives are less open to criticism.

Setting military figures aside, we find many transformational leaders whose past sacrifice serves as a strong foundation for subsequent efforts to influence and persuade. The Burmese activist Aung San Suu Kyi comes to mind. As, of course, does the man I mentioned briefly in the opening lecture of this course, Nelson Mandela. As a leading figure in the African National Congress, the ANC, Mandela had stood in opposition to the racist apartheid system since its inception in 1948. Initially, he favored nonviolent tactics, but in the face of ongoing repression, he changed his mind. In 1955 he claimed publicly that the ANC had "no alternative to armed and violent resistance."

This decision, and his subsequent actions, led to Mandela's arrest in 1962 and the banning of the ANC as a political party. In 1964 Mandela was found guilty of conspiracy to overthrow the government and was sentenced to life in prison. Mandela was initially imprisoned in a concrete cell measuring seven by eight feet and spent his days in hard labor. Even so, he stayed politically active and was involved in politicking and hunger strikes. In total, Mandela spent 27 years in prison, where he suffered permanent damage to his eyesight and at one point caught tuberculosis. But he also continued to build a reputation and learn, earning a law degree and learning Afrikaans, the language spoken by the whites in South Africa.

In 1990, the new white leader of South Africa, Frederik de Klerk, decided that apartheid was unsustainable, and he met with Mandela. After the meeting, de Klerk freed Mandela unconditionally, and lifted the ban on the ANC. Much of the ensuing two years was spent in formal negotiation between de Klerk's government and Mandela's ANC as they attempted to dismantle apartheid. A free election, with whites and blacks free to vote, was set for April 1994. Given that the vast majority of the South African population is black, it wasn't a surprise that Mandela was elected President and began work on what many consider to be his lasting legacy.

Although Mandela had embraced violence earlier in his life, he came out strongly for national reconciliation. He used inspirational language and set himself up as a role model. He referred to South Africa as the Rainbow Nation and brought whites into his governing cabinet. He also sought to bring the nation together by convincing blacks to get behind the national rugby team, the Springboks, which up until that time had been despised by blacks. In a series of events made famous by movies like *Invictus*, Mandela used rugby as a symbol of reconciliation. And when South Africa won the Rugby World Cup in 1995, he actually presented the championship trophy to captain Francois Pienaar while wearing a Springboks jersey.

Recall from Yorges' work that sacrifices make leaders even more influential. In Mandela's case, he had sacrificed nearly everything to the advancement of political rights for blacks in South Africa. Following the collapse of apartheid, there were some who called for war and justice by jailing the oppressors. Mandela, however, had a higher goal in mind. And largely because of his credibility, his reputation, and stature as a man who had sacrificed for the cause, he was able to convince his countrymen to join him in pursuit of that higher goal. He used inspirational motivation by focusing attention on symbols of unity, like the Rainbow and the Springbok jersey. And he used idealized influence by modeling forgiveness, forgiving the politicians, and even the jailers who held him captive over those many years. Were it not for Mandela's transformational leadership, South Africa may well have descended into civil war rather than move peacefully forward toward national unity and economic prosperity.

Mandela is a fantastic example of just how much is possible with transformational leadership. Transformational leaders establish a vision and use all the influence tactics they can to encourage others to join them in pursuit. Not many of us have sacrificed the way that Mandela sacrificed, but it is still possible to use your past history to convince people that your motives are good ones when you go to lead.

I remember a senior administrator who interviewed at the University of Iowa a while back. He came to interview from the West Coast, after having been a senior administrator at three other universities. To some of us, it felt a bit like he was just working his way up the ladder by moving wherever there were job openings. How did he convince people that his motives for coming to Iowa were something more than just personal ambition?

What he did was tell a story about how his first exposure to the United States was when he attended Grinnell College as an undergraduate, and how the people of Iowa made him feel welcome, and how Iowa became to him like a second home. So, to come back and be an administrator at the University of Iowa was, he told us, like coming home again. It would be an opportunity to return the remarkable hospitality he had received as a student. Clearly, attending Grinnell, which is a fantastic liberal arts college about an hour from the University of Iowa, was not a personal sacrifice on his part, but this is a really useful story. This administrator's Grinnell story provided some evidence that his motives for wanting to be a leader at the University of Iowa were not purely selfish. They were driven by a calling to come home and give back. So the point is you don't have to go prison to establish yourself as a credible transformational leader. Look to your own personal history for stories that you can use to draw out and convince others of your better motives.

So far we've discussed transformational leadership in some detail, beginning with former CEO Ray Anderson and continuing with former South African President Nelson Mandela. Now let's talk about two things you can do to practice influence the way that transformational leaders do it. First, consider an issue or cause that's personally important to you. Are you passionate about the need for more public land in your city or town? Do you think local property taxes are too high? Does the local animal shelter need to expand and buy a new facility? In each case, there is an opportunity for someone like you to be transformative. So, pick your cause; reach out to others; build relationships based on common values, interests, and principles; establish a shared vision; and mobilize people to make it happen.

What if you don't want to give speeches or act as the formal spokesperson for your chosen cause? Is there another way that you can move forward the ideas in this lecture? Yes, and that leads us to my second suggestion. You can design and plan the influence campaign. To mobilize people's hearts and minds, you can help decide on the ideals and symbols, the stories and the particular figureheads that will win people over. So your task is to help prepare the influence campaign that must accompany your group's efforts. You may not be the one to deliver the speeches, but you can help build its components, the logos, as we discussed in our lecture on speech building, and the vision and symbols, as we've discussed today.

Whether as a leader or part of a team, are you ready to use influence to make a change in the world around you? It has been a privilege and a whole lot of fun to be with you over the course of these last 12 lectures. I hope that you've learned something that will help you right away. Perhaps what you've learned about the four key factors of influence, agent, target, tactics, and context, perhaps that knowledge will help you the next time you're bombarded with influence attempts from advertisers and sales people. Perhaps keeping the ATTiC acronym in mind, you'll make sure that you are buying what you really need and not what you've been lured into buying. Perhaps it will help you avoid being taken advantage of by someone with negative characteristics of narcissism, Machiavellianism, or psychopathy.

More positively, I hope you will be better at selling your own ideas, in speeches, interviews, and at the negotiating table. Above all, I hope that what I've talked about here will inspire you. I hope it will inspire you to give transformational leadership a try. By mastering the underlying mechanisms of influence, you are now better prepared to be a transformative force, to change things that happen in your homes, your businesses, and your communities. So I encourage—I challenge you—to put what you've learned about influence to use on behalf of a cause that is near and dear to your heart.

Bibliography

Allgeier, Sandy. *The Personal Credibility Factor: How to Get It, Keep It, and Get It Back (If You've Lost It)*. Upper Saddle River, NJ: Pearson Education, 2009. Practical advice on how to become more credible in your day-to-day interactions.

Anderson, Ray C. *Mid-Course Correction: Toward a Sustainable Enterprise: The Interface Model*. Atlanta: Peregrinzilla Press, 1999. The story of how Ray Anderson became concerned about the environment and the changes he made in the way his company does business to promote sustainability.

Antonakis, John, Marika Fenley, and Sue Liechti. "Can Charisma Be Taught? Tests of Two Interventions." *Academy of Management Learning and Education* 10, no. 3 (2011): 374–396. Two studies showing that with training, people can become more charismatic in how they interact with others and give speeches.

Asch, Solomon E. "Effects of Group Pressure on the Modification and Distortion of Judgment." In *Readings in Social Psychology*, edited by E. E. Maccoby, T. M. Newcomb, and E. L. Hartley. New York: Holt, Rinehart, & Winston, 1958. A summary of Asch's studies on conformity using the line judgment task.

———. "Studies of Independence and Conformity: A Minority of One against a Unanimous Majority." *Psychological Monographs* 70, no. 9 (1956): 1–70. The original publication describing experiments with the line judgment task. Under a variety of conditions, individuals conform and agree with the group opinion.

Attkisson, Sharyl. "Fraud Convictions after CBS News Investigation of 'Storm Chasers.'" CBS News, March 26, 2012. http://www.cbsnews.com/8301-31727_162-57404811-10391695/fraud-convictions-after-cbs-news-investigation-of-storm-chasers. Describes the crimes of Dominik Sadowski, a contractor convicted of insurance fraud.

Babiak, Paul, and Robert D. Hare. *Snakes in Suits: When Psychopaths Go to Work*. New York: Regan Books, 2006. A look at Hare's work on psychopathy as applied to work settings.

Bacon, John U. *Three and Out: Rich Rodriguez and the Michigan Wolverines in the Crucible of College Football*. New York: Farrar, Straus and Giroux, 2011. The story of Rich Rodriguez's three seasons as head coach of the University of Michigan men's football team.

Barling, Julian, Tom Weber, and E. Kevin Kelloway. "Effects of Transformational Leadership Training on Attitudinal and Financial Outcomes: A Field Experiment." *Journal of Applied Psychology* 81, no. 6 (1996): 827–832. Field study showing that training in transformational leadership boosted the leadership behaviors of participants and the work outcomes of their employees.

Bass, Bernard M., and Bruce J. Avolio. *Improving Organizational Effectiveness through Transformational Leadership*. Thousand Oaks, CA: Sage, 1994. The seminal introduction of Burns's transformational leadership theory into the study of business leadership.

Billig, M., and Henri Tajfel. "Social Categorization and Similarity in Intergroup Behavior." *European Journal of Social Psychology* 3, no. 3 (1973): 27–51. A study demonstrating that even random assignment into groups can result in discrimination.

Bolino, Mark C., and William H. Turnley. "More Than One Way to Make an Impression: Exploring Profiles in Impression Management." *Journal of Management* 29, no. 2 (2003): 141–160. A set of studies showing how students use impression management tactics during group projects.

Bond, Rod, and Peter B. Smith. "Culture and Conformity: A Meta-Analysis of Studies Using Asch's (1952b, 1956) Line Judgment Task." *Psychological Bulletin* 119, no. 1 (1996): 111–137. This meta-analysis of Asch's study, discussed in Lecture 1, also investigates the relationship between conformity and individualism/collectivism.

Brüne, Martin, Cumhur Tas, Julia Wischniewski, Anna Welpinghus, Christine Heinisch, and Albert Newen. "Hypnotic Ingroup-Outgroup Suggestion Influences Economic Decision Making in an Ultimatum Game." *Consciousness and Cognition* 21, no. 2 (2012): 939–946. A study examining who accepts unfair offers in the classic ultimatum game.

Burger, Jerry M. "Replicating Milgram: Would People Still Obey Today?" *American Psychologist* 64, no. 1 (2009): 1–11. This paper describes the partial replication of Milgram's classic study. There are a few commentaries, some of them critical, published in the same issue.

Burger, Jerry M., Nicole Messian, Shebani Patel, Alicia del Prado, and Carmen Anderson. "What a Coincidence! The Effects of Incidental Similarity on Compliance." *Personality and Social Psychology Bulletin* 30, no. 1 (2004): 35–43. A series of studies showing how incidental similarity increases compliance with a request.

Burger, Jerry M., Jackeline Sanchez, Jenny E. Imberi, and Lucia R. Grande. "The Norm of Reciprocity as an Internalized Social Norm: Returning Favors Even When No One Finds Out." *Social Influence* 4, no. 1 (2009): 11–17. An experiment demonstrating that people will pay back a small favor even if the person who provided the favor won't know.

Burns, James MacGregor. *Leadership*. Reprint ed. New York: Harper Perennial Political Classics, 2010. Ever the political historian, Burns uses historical leaders to propose a new theory of leadership.

Cabane, Olivia Fox. *The Charisma Myth: How Anyone Can Master the Art and Science of Personal Magnetism*. New York: Penguin, 2012. A book with specific guidance on how anyone can learn to appear charismatic to others.

Carnegie, Dale. *How to Win Friends and Influence People*. Reissue ed. New York: Simon & Schuster, 2009. This is the classic, but Dale Carnegie Associates has released updates, and there are volumes that bundle this book with his other works. Also, for a summary of specific public speaking tips, see Carnegie and Associates, "Speak More Effectively by Dale Carnegie,

Part One: Public Speaking a Quick and Easy Way," http://www.dalecarnegie. com.

Cialdini, Robert B. *Influence: Science and Practice*. New York: Pearson, 2008. What many consider to be the most comprehensive book on influence. Cialdini has written related books and has an extensive website with videos (http://www.influenceatwork.com).

Cohen, Herb. *You Can Negotiate Anything*. Secaucus, NJ: Lyle Stuart, 1980. Useful reading to supplement Lecture 11.

Davies, James C. "Toward a Theory of Revolution." *American Sociological Review* 27, no. 1 (1962): 5–19. In this article, Davies advances his J theory of political revolutions.

De Dreu, Carsten K. W. "Time Pressure and the Closing of the Mind in Negotiation." *Organizational Behavior and Human Decision Processes* 91, no. 2 (2003): 280–295. Two studies showing how time pressure influences negotiation processes and outcomes.

Denburg, Natalie L., Catherine A. Cole, Michael Hernandez, Torricia H. Yamada, Daniel Tranel, Antoine Bechara, and Robert B. Wallace. "The Orbitofrontal Cortex, Real-World Decision Making, and Normal Aging. *Annals of the New York Academy of Sciences*, 1121 (2007): 480–498. Presents three studies showing the reasoning deficits that lead older adults to be susceptible to deceptive advertising.

Dutton, Kevin. *Split-Second Persuasion: The Ancient Art and New Science of Changing Minds*. New York: Houghton Mifflin Harcourt, 2011. Although Dutton's book overlaps with Cialdini's in some ways, he offers additional insights.

Ellis, Aleksander P. J., Bradley J. West, Ann Marie Ryan, and Richard P. DeShon. "The Use of Impression Management Tactics in Structured Interviews: A Function of Question Type?" *Journal of Applied Psychology* 87, no. 6 (2002): 1200–1208. A study examining impression management tactics used in a structured interview setting.

Ferris, Gerald R., Darren C. Treadway, Robert W. Kolodinsky, Wayne A. Hochwarter, Charles J. Kacmar, Ceasar Douglas, and Dwight D. Frink. "Development and Validation of a Political Skill Inventory." *Journal of Management* 31, no. 1 (2005): 126–152. Studies that describe the rationale behind, and the development of, a survey measure of political skill in organizations.

Fisher, Roger, William Ury, and Bruce Patton. *Getting to Yes: Negotiating Agreement without Giving In.* 2nd ed. New York: Penguin, 1991. A classic text that distinguishes between position-based and principle-based negotiation and describes how principled negotiation works to satisfy both parties.

French, John R. P., and Bertram Raven. "The Bases of Social Power." In *Studies in Social Power*, edited by Dorwin Cartwright, pp. 259–269. Ann Arbor: University of Michigan Press, 1959. The original chapter that outlines five bases of power.

Gaertner, Lowell, and Chester A. Insko. "Intergroup Discrimination in the Minimal Group Paradigm: Categorization, Reciprocation, or Fear?" *Journal of Personality and Social Psychology* 79, no. 1 (2000): 77–94. Two studies that replicate and extend the minimal-group paradigm established by Henri Tajfel. They demonstrate that in-group favoritism is more likely when group members were reliant on one another and could return the favor.

Galin, Amira, Miron Gross, and Gavriel Gosalker. "E-negotiation Versus Face-to-Face Negotiation: What Has Changed—If Anything?" *Computers in Human Behavior* 23, no. 1 (2007): 787–797. An experiment comparing face-to-face and e-mail negotiations in terms of both tactics and outcomes.

Greenspan, Stephen. *Annals of Gullibility: Why We Get Duped and How to Avoid It.* Westport, CT: Praeger, 2009. A review of gullibility stories that culminates with a theory about why people are sometimes so easily convinced.

Heinrichs, Jay. *Thank You for Arguing: What Aristotle, Lincoln, and Homer Simpson Can Teach Us about the Art of Persuasion.* New York: Three Rivers Press, 2007. An engaging tour through the history of rhetoric, with many practical examples. You can also visit his blog at http://inpraiseofargument. squarespace.com.

Henriques, Diana B. *The Wizard of Lies: Bernie Madoff and the Death of Trust.* New York: Times Books, 2011. A thorough telling of the rise and fall of Bernie Madoff.

Higgins, C. A., Timothy A. Judge, and Gerald R. Ferris. "Influence Tactics and Work Outcomes: A Meta-Analysis." *Journal of Organizational Behavior* 24 (2003): 89–106. Examines 31 studies to determine the relationship between influence tactics and work outcomes of performance and extrinsic success.

Holoien, Deborah Son, and Susan T. Fiske. "Downplaying Positive Impressions: Compensation between Warmth and Competence in Impression Management." *Journal of Experimental Social Psychology* 49, no. 1 (2013): 33–41. Examines how students asked to write notes trade off between making impressions of warmth and of competence, depending on the instructions given.

Jonason, Peter K., Sarah Slomski, and Jamie Partyka. "The Dark Triad at Work: How Toxic Employees Get Their Way." *Personality and Individual Differences* 52, no. 3 (2012): 449–453. Large survey study examining correlations among dark triad personality characteristics and the use of influence tactics.

Jonason, Peter K., and Gregory D. Webster. "The Dirty Dozen: A Concise Measure of the Dark Triad." *Psychological Assessment* 22, no. 2 (2010): 420–432. Describes the development of a 12-item measure of the three negative personality traits of narcissism, Machiavellianism, and psychopathy.

Judge, Timothy A., and Robert D. Bretz. "Political Influence Behavior and Career Success." *Journal of Management* 20, no. 1 (1994): 43–65. A field study examining the relationship among supervisor-focused and self-focused influence tactics on career outcomes.

Judge, Timothy A., and Ronald F. Piccolo. "Transformational and Transactional Leadership: A Meta-Analytic Test of Their Relative Validity." *Journal of Applied Psychology* 89, no. 5 (2004): 755–768. A synthesis of studies showing that transformational leadership has strong relationships with work-related outcomes, including satisfaction with the leader, motivation, and perceived leader effectiveness.

Kotov, Roman I., S. B. Bellman, and David B. Watson. *Multidimensional Iowa Suggestibility Scale (MISS) Brief Manual.* medicine. stonybrookmedicine.edu/system/files/MISSBriefManual.pdf. Accessed May 14, 2013. A description of the development and validation of a survey measure of suggestibility.

Langlois, Judith H., Lisa Kalakanis, Adam J. Rubenstein, Andrea Larson, Monica Hallam, and Monica Smoot. "Maxims or Myths of Beauty? A Meta-Analytic and Theoretical Review." *Psychological Bulletin* 126, no. 3 (2000): 390–423. Reviews 67 studies on judgments of beauty and their correlates.

Latané, Bibb, and John M. Darley. *The Unresponsive Bystander: Why Doesn't He Help?* New York: Appleton-Century-Crofts, 1970. A description of experiments about bystander intervention, including studies conducted on the streets of New York City.

Leistico, Anne-Marie R., Randall T. Salekin, Jamie DeCoster, and Richard Rogers. "A Large-Scale Meta-Analysis Relating Hare Measures of Psychopathy to Antisocial Conduct." *Law and Human Behavior* 32, no. 1 (2008): 28–45. Examines 95 studies to determine the relationship between the Hare checklist and various types of problematic behavior.

"LouisianREBUILDS.info Contractor Fraud Survey Results." http://www. gnoinfo.com/files/Survey.pdf. Accessed May 14, 2013. Survey results that explain the nature and scope of contractor fraud following the Katrina recovery efforts in New Orleans.

Lynn, Michael. "Increasing Servers' Tips: What Managers Can Do and Why They Should Do It." *Journal of Foodservice Business Research* 8, no. 4 (2005): 89–98. A review of literature on how to increase servers' tips.

Mandela, Nelson. *Long Walk to Freedom: The Autobiography of Nelson Mandela.* New York: Little, Brown & Co., 1995. One of many books on Mandela, this is his own version of his early life and efforts to lead post-apartheid South Africa.

Milgram, Stanley. *Obedience to Authority: An Experimental View.* New York: Harper & Row, 1974. This book describes the series of obedience studies Milgram conducted in the 1960s.

Mullaney, Kevin. "Leader Influence Behavior from the Target's Perspective: A Two-Factor Model." Master's thesis, University of Illinois Urbana-Champaign, 2011. A thorough study of the relationships among influence tactics and their outcomes.

Padilla, Art, Robert Hogan, and Robert B. Kaiser, "The Toxic Triangle: Destructive Leaders, Susceptible Followers, and Conducive Environments." *The Leadership Quarterly* 18 (2007): 176–194. Argues for three factors that combine to create destructive leadership—characteristics of leaders, characteristics of followers, and context—and illustrates the combination by examining Fidel Castro's leadership in Cuba.

Park, Sun Hyun, James D. Westphal, and Ithai Stern. "Set up for a Fall: The Insidious Effects of Flattery and Opinion Conformity toward Corporate Leaders." *Administrative Science Quarterly* 56, no. 2 (2011): 257–302. A study of CEOs, showing that they fall victim to flattery and persist in pursuing a losing strategy.

Petty, Richard E., and John T. Cacioppo. *Communication and Persuasion: Central and Peripheral Routes to Attitude Change.* New York: Springer-Verlag, 1986. A classic book describing a dual-channel theory of attitude change.

Petty, Richard E., John T. Cacioppo, and David Schumann. "Central and Peripheral Routes to Advertising Effectiveness: The Moderating Role of Involvement." *Journal of Consumer Research* 10 (1983): 135–146. The seminal article demonstrating that argument quality had a greater impact on product attitudes when research participants were paying close attention.

Pfeffer, Jeffrey. *Power: Why Some People Have It and Others Don't.* New York: HarperCollins, 2010. A business trade book that reviews research on power and offers specific suggestions for how to increase your own power at work.

Pink, Daniel. *To Sell Is Human: The Surprising Truth about Moving Others.* New York: Riverhead Books, 2012. An intriguing look at research and practice on selling, in the broadest sense of the term.

Pugh, S. Doug. "Service with a Smile: Emotional Contagion in the Service Encounter." *Academy of Management Journal* 44, no. 5 (2001): 1018–1027. A field study demonstrating the effect of smiling on service encounters.

Rezlescu, Constantin, Brad Duchaine, Christopher Y. Olivola, and Nick Chater. "Unfakeable Facial Configurations Affect Strategic Choices in Trust Games with or without Information about Past Behavior." *PLOS One* 7, no. 3 (2012): e34293. Three studies that examine features of faces that determine trustworthiness, along with how people react to those faces. The online article is open source and includes free pictures and graphics.

Ronson, Jon. *The Psychopath Test: A Journey through the Madness Industry.* London: Macmillan, 2011. Ronson digs deeper into Hare's psychopathy checklist and interviews Al Dunlap along the way.

Schneider, Andrea Kupfer. "Shattering Negotiation Myths: Empirical Evidence on the Effectiveness of Negotiation Style." *Harvard Negotiation Law Review* 143 (2002): 143–233. Schneider asks lawyers about tactics used in negotiation contexts and challenges the notion that an adversarial approach is more effective than a more cooperative, problem-solving approach.

Sherif, Muzafer, O. J. Harvey, B. Jack White, William R. Hood, and Carolyn W. Sherif. *The Robbers Cave Experiment: Intergroup Conflict and Cooperation.* Norman, OK: The University Book Exchange. 1954. A thorough description of the classic Robbers Cave Experiment, which demonstrates how conflict occurs as a natural result of dividing people into separate groups.

Skeem, Jennifer L., and David J. Cooke. "Is Criminal Behavior a Central Component of Psychopathy? Conceptual Directions for Resolving the Debate." *Psychological Assessment* 22, no. 2 (2010): 433–445. An argument critical of some uses of the Hare checklist, arguing for stronger distinctions between constructs (psychopathy) and imperfect measures of those constructs (the Hare checklist).

Spitzer, Manfred, Urs Fischbacher, Bärbel Herrnberger, Georg Grön, and Ernst Ferh. "The Neural Signature of Social Norm Compliance." *Neuron* 56 (2007): 185–196. Researchers used functional MRI to examine brains of participants playing a game in which they could either be punished or not for violating a norm. Differences in neural activation were found between high- and low-Machiavellian participants.

Stewart, Greg L., Susan L. Dustin, Murray R. Barrick, and Todd C. Darnold. "Exploring the Handshake in Employment Interviews." *Journal of Applied Psychology* 93, no. 5 (2008): 1139–1146. A study showing that interviewees with firmer handshakes received higher employability ratings.

Sullivan, Brandon M., Kathleen M. O'Connor, and Ethan R. Burris. "Negotiator Confidence: The Impact of Self-Efficacy on Tactics and Outcomes." *Journal of Experimental Social Psychology* 42, no. 5 (2006): 567–581. A study demonstrating that confidence in the various components of principle-based negotiation predicts the adoption of this approach.

Tajfel, Henri. "Experiments in Intergroup Discrimination." *Scientific American* 223, no. 2 (1970): 96–102. Reports a series of studies showing that grouping people results in different behavior toward ingroup and outgroup members.

Tajfel, Henri, M. G. Billig, R. P. Bundy, and Claude Flament. "Social Categorization and Intergroup Behaviour." *European Journal of Social Psychology* 1, no. 2 (1971): 149–177. Two studies showing the power of assignment to groups in determining intergroup discrimination.

Triandis, H. *Individualism and Collectivism*. Boulder, CO: Westview Press, 1995. A monograph that discusses the key attributes and outcomes of these two cultural constructs.

Westphal, James D., and David L. Deephouse. "Avoiding Bad Press: Interpersonal Influence in Relations between CEOs and Journalists and the Consequences for Press Reporting about Firms and Their Leadership." *Organization Science* 22, no. 4 (2011): 1061–1086. A study showing the connection between CEO use of ingratiation and reporters' explanations of why their companies did or did not have earnings that met expectations. Reporters who had been recipients of ingratiation attempts were more likely to attribute failure to meet earnings to the economy rather than to company leadership.

Xie, Guang-Xin, and David M. Boush. "How Susceptible Are Consumers to Deceptive Advertising Claims? A Retrospective Look at the Experimental Research Literature." *The Marketing Review* 11, no. 3 (2011): 293–314. A review of prior literature indicating, among other findings, that older adults are more susceptible to deceptive advertising.

Yukl, Gary, Helen Kim, and Cecilia M. Falbe. "Antecedents of Influence Outcomes." *Journal of Applied Psychology* 81, no. 3 (1996): 309–317. Examines the factors that lead to target commitment.

Yukl, Gary, and Rubina Mahsud. "Why Flexible and Adaptive Leadership Is Essential." *Consulting Psychology Journal: Practice and Research* 62, no. 2 (2010): 81–93. The authors argue that effective leaders are flexible in their use of influence tactics and other leadership behaviors, adapting to the immediate situation.

Bibliography